MAORI MYTH AND LEGEND

MAORI MYTH AND LEGEND

illustrated by Roger Hart
with text by A. W. Reed

REED

First published separately as
Maori Legends, 1972, and *Maori Myth*, 1977

This combined and revised edition published 1983

A. H. & A. W. REED LTD
68–74 Kingsford Smith Street, Wellington 3
also

7 Kirk Street, Auckland 2
85 Thackeray Street, Christchurch 2

ISBN 0 589 01471 4

Typeset by Quickset, Christchurch
Printed by Kyodo-Shing Loong Printing Industries Pte, Ltd, Singapore

CONTENTS

Maui-potiki and his brothers snare Tama-nui-te-ra (*see page 27*)

AUTHOR'S INTRODUCTION

The gods of Aotearoa are found in many islands of Polynesia, but in no other place were the cosmogony and pantheon of gods more clearly and imaginatively defined than among the Maori people, who lived close to nature and endued their surroundings with unending variety of personifications of natural phenomena – personifications that were the descendants of the departmental gods who controlled earth, sea and sky.

The Maori peopled their world, the Ao-marama, or "World of Light", with such gods and manifestations. They had their own vivid account of the creation of the world, the separation of earth and sky, the clothing of the Earth Mother, and the ornamenting of the Sky Father with sun, moon, and stars by Tane-matua.

Natural and supernatural phenomena are interwoven in the several aspects of Maori culture, not only in myth, legend, and incantation, but also in song and dance. Those who are familiar with the myths of Polynesia will be aware that the Maori of New Zealand were fortunate in their heritage of gods. But they were also individualist, even radical in their views. Tradition was sacred but not immutable. While their departmental gods retained the names and functions ascribed to them by their Polynesian ancestors their relative importance was changed, and for valid reasons. Living on smaller islands than their New Zealand descendants (in some cases even on atolls) the sea was all important to the Pacific Islanders as the source of food and therefore of life. Tangaroa, the god of the sea, naturally became the most important of their departmental gods.

Although no part of New Zealand is more than a hundred and thirty kilometres from the sea the land area was far greater than the largest Polynesian island group. Forested hills and plains provided birds, vegetable food, and eels and fish in greater profusion and variety than the sea. As the guardian of trees and, by inference, of all terrestrial phenomena, Tane therefore became the foremost departmental god of the Maori; the benefactor of the Maori people; the progenitor of life itself. As the ocean waves battered the shore, the supernatural guardians were naturally at enmity with each other and jointly against Tawhiri-matea, the god of wind, whose allegiance was with the Sky Father rather than with the Earth Mother.

These were noble, wide-ranging concepts. Dependence on the supernatural representatives of life-sustaining forces is nowhere more clearly exemplified than in the elevation of Haumia-tiketike, the guardian of the humble but necessary bracken rhizome, to departmental rank along with his more flamboyant brethren.

The adventures of the gods had an important influence on thought and custom, and provided assurance that man and his surroundings were under the guardianship of supernatural forces that were prepared to protect those who honoured them.

In more homely mood there were tender stories of love and endurance, tales of monsters and ghostly creatures of the night and the mist-enshrouded forests, together with firm belief in an after-life. There were many atua, deities to be appealed to in time of war or crisis, and enchanted logs and stones that possessed magical qualities. The inner recesses of the forest were peopled with fairy-like folk, supernatural animals preyed on humans, and malignant sea creatures invaded the land by night.

Natural phenomena were explained by tales of ingenious invention. There were many stories of the sun, moon and stars. Mountains, rivers and lakes were given names and characters and frequently acted as human beings, as also did the trees and forest plants, the wind and the weather.

There were fearsome revelations of the evil powers of wizards, tales of flying men, giants, witches and wild men of the forest. In the field of human activity there were stories of cultivation and home-making, voyages and journeys on sea and land, the playing of games, fishing, hunting, and waging of relentless wars.

In compiling the text, the author has adapted many of the legends from his earlier, comprehensive volume *Treasury of Maori Folklore*, and to a lesser extent the more popular *Myths and Legends of Maoriland*.

A. W. REED

ARTIST'S INTRODUCTION

Myths, legends and folk tales seem always to spring from and retain the characteristics of the landscapes of their origins. So, the Black Forests of Germany automatically conjure up images of the Brothers Grimm; the soft twilights of Scotland evoke Celtic folklore and the tales of Bonnie Prince Charlie; the harsh expanses of Australia give immediate meaning to the Aboriginal stories of earth, fire and water.

Thus the New Zealand landscape, different from these, lends its own characteristics to the legends of the Maori; stories of trees, mountains, lakes, demons, fairies, underworlds and overworlds, and all manner of phenomena that affected their daily existence.

It is from this viewpoint that I have illustrated this book – the figures are to be seen as part of the landscape, whatever it is that may be happening to them. The landscapes are mostly real, be they with or without figures, and represent places which are, for me, very strong in their evocations of legendary and supernatural occurrences.

Such is Lake Waikaremoana, which forms the background to several of the illustrations. When the mists descend, and all is grey and still, the concept of patupaiarehe and taniwha, ogresses and giant birds become more than real; one becomes aware of pervasive forces very different from those of the Pakeha, and no doubt only fully understood by the Maori. However, it is this world, through the medium of paint and ink, that I have perhaps foolishly tried to enter.

ROGER HART

THE CREATION

Listen to the chants of creation

Lift, lift up the south land.
Upward, upward lift the south sky.
Put each in its own position
There to rest for ever.
Lift, lift up Rangi,
And with offering made to thee, O Rangi,
We lift thee up!

Stand apart the skin,
Be divided the skin,
As the nettle to the skin,
As the tataramoa to the skin.
Do not grieve for your partner,
Do not cry for your husband.
Let the ocean be broken,
Let the ocean be far apart;
Be you united to the sea,
Yes, to the sea, O earth;
Broken asunder are you two.
Do not grieve,
Do not continue your love,
Do not grieve for your partner.

In the beginning was Te Kore, the Nothing, and from Te Kore came Te Po, the Night. In that impenetrable darkness Rangi the Sky Father lay in the arms of Papa the Earth Mother.

The gods, who were their children, crawled through the narrow space between their clinging bodies. They longed for freedom, for wind blowing over sharp hill tops and deep valleys, and light to warm their pale bodies.

"What can we do?" they asked. "We need room to stretch our cramped limbs. We need light. We need space."

Then Tane-mahuta, mighty father of the forest, father of all living things that love light and freedom, rose to his feet. For as long as a man can hold his breath Tane stood, silent and unmoving, summoning all his strength. He pressed his hands against the body of his mother and turning upside-down he planted his feet firmly on his father. He straightened his back and pushed against Rangi.

The primal parents clung to each other. Tane exerted all his strength, straining back and limbs, until at last the mighty bodies of earth and sky were forced apart.

"It was the fierce thrusting of Tane that tore the heaven from the earth," was an ancient saying of the Maori people. "So they were sent apart, and darkness was made manifest, and so was the light."

Rangi was hurled far away while angry winds screamed through the space between earth and sky.

Tane and his brothers looked at the soft curves of their mother. As the light crept across the land they saw a veil of silver mist that hung over her naked shoulders — the mist of grief for her lost husband. Tears dropped fast from Rangi's eyes. The showers of rain ran together in pools and streams across the body of Papa.

Although he had separated his parents so forcibly, Tane loved them both. He set to work to clothe his mother in beauty that had not been dreamed of in the dark world. He brought his own children, the trees, and set them in the earth. But Tane was like a child learning by trial and error the wisdom that had not yet been born. He planted the trees upside down. Their heads were buried in the soil, while the bare white roots remained stiff and unmoving in the breeze.

It was no place for his other children, the birds and the insects. He pulled up a giant kauri tree, shook the soil from the branches, set the roots firmly in the ground, and proudly surveyed the spreading crown set above the clean, straight trunk. The breeze played with the leaves, singing the song of a new world.

The earth lay still and beautiful, wrapped in a cloak of living green. The ocean lapped her body, the birds and the insects ran and fluttered in the fresh breeze. The brown-skinned gods frolicked under the leaves of the garden of Tane. Each had a duty to perform. Rongo-ma-tane preserved the fertility of the growing things of earth. Haumia-tiketike tended the humble fernroot. Tu-matauenga was the god of war. Tangaroa controlled the restless waves. Only one of the seventy brothers left the placid shelter of his mother to follow his father. It was Tawhiri-matea, the god of all the winds that blow between earth and sky.

Tane-mahuta raised his eyes to where Rangi lay, cold and grey and unlovely in the vast spaces above the earth and was sorry for the desolation of his father. He took the bright sun and placed it on Rangi's back with the silver moon in front. He travelled through the ten heavens until he found a garment of glowing red. After that he rested for seven days, and then spread the cloak across the sky from east to west and north to south.

But Tane was not satisfied. He decided that the gift was not worthy of his father and stripped it off. A small piece remained, a fragment of the garment men still see at the time of the setting sun.

"Great father," Tane cried, "in the long dark nights before Marama the moon shines on your breast, all things sorrow. I will journey to the very ends of space to find adornment for you."

Somewhere in the silence he heard an answering sigh. He passed swiftly to the very end of the world, into the darkness, until he reached Maunganui, the Great Mountain, where the Shining Ones lived. They were children of Uru, Tane-mahuta's brother. The two brothers watched them playing at the foot of the mountain.

Tane begged Uru to give him some of the shining lights to fasten on the mantle of the sky. Uru rose to his feet and gave a great shout. The Shining Ones heard and came rolling up the slope to their father. Uru placed a basket in front of Tane. He plunged his arms into the glowing mass of lights and piled the Shining Ones into the basket.

Tane placed five glowing lights in the shape of a cross on the breast of Rangi and sprinkled the dark blue robe with the Children of Light. The basket he hung in the wide heavens. It is the basket of the Milky Way. Sometimes Uru's children tumble and fall swiftly towards the earth, but for the most part they remain like fireflies on the mantle of the night sky.

THE COMING
OF KNOWLEDGE

The task of passing sacred lore from one generation to another was entrusted to the tohunga ahurewa, the medium of the gods. He was the expert in makutu (witchcraft), tapu (sacerdotal restrictions), and karakia (incantations). The tohunga was responsible for passing on the knowledge he had gained from his predecessors and was required to practise it throughout his active life.

The school at which tohunga were trained was the whare wananga (house of occult knowledge). There were several grades, the highest of which was the whare kura (school of learning) in which historical traditions, legends, and the ritual of war and agriculture, as well as the deeper mysteries of their craft, were taught. In a metaphysical sense sacred knowledge was enshrined in stones known as whatukura and which were contained in the "baskets of knowledge". There were three baskets, the kete-aronui, with beneficial knowledge, the kete-tuauri, with the full range of ritual and incantation, and the kete-tuatea, containing the knowledge of evil and black magic.

The three baskets were brought from the overworlds to earth by the god Tane. During the nineteenth century the basic account of Tane's bold sortie into the overworlds may have been influenced by Christian concepts of good and evil, as personified by Tane and Whiro. It is reasonably certain, however, that Tane was responsible for obtaining this gift to mankind at great risk to himself.

Tane was not the only god who aspired to obtain the priceless gift but after much dissension and chicanery Tane was the one chosen to ascend the overworlds in quest of the sacred lore. He had the foresight to select a suitable site for the first earthly whare kura in which the baskets were to be enshrined.

He then ascended to Rangi-tamaku, the second overworld, where he found a pattern for the whare wananga, which he copied on his return to earth. Tane ascended on the swaying ropes that were the rising whirlwinds of Tawhiri-matea. Whiro, who also aspired to the honour, followed his brother by a more circuitous route along the fringes of the several overworlds. On his arrival at Rangi-tamaku he learnt that Tane was in the next overworld and sent his "hordes" to attack him. It was a combined operation of mosquitoes, sandflies, owls, bats, and other nocturnal creatures. It would have gone badly with Tane if Tawhiri-matea's whirlwinds had not scattered them to the far corners of heaven.

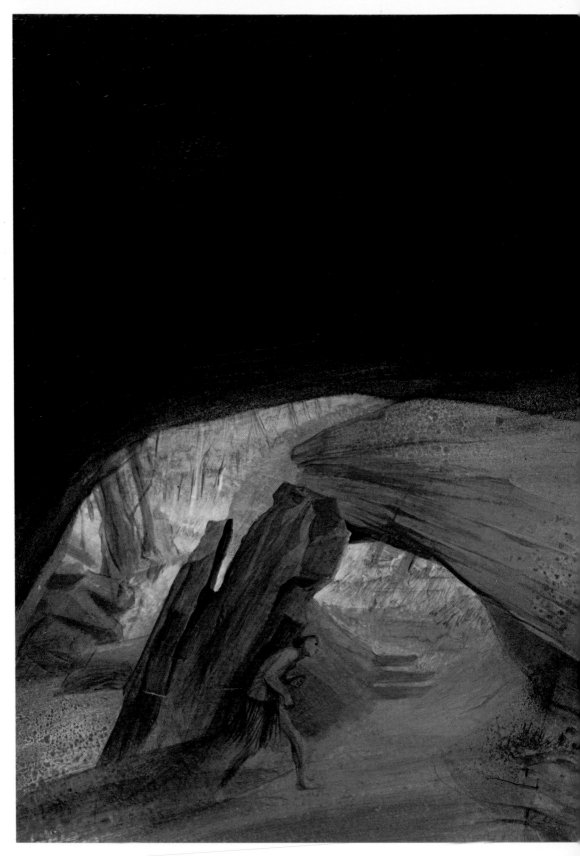

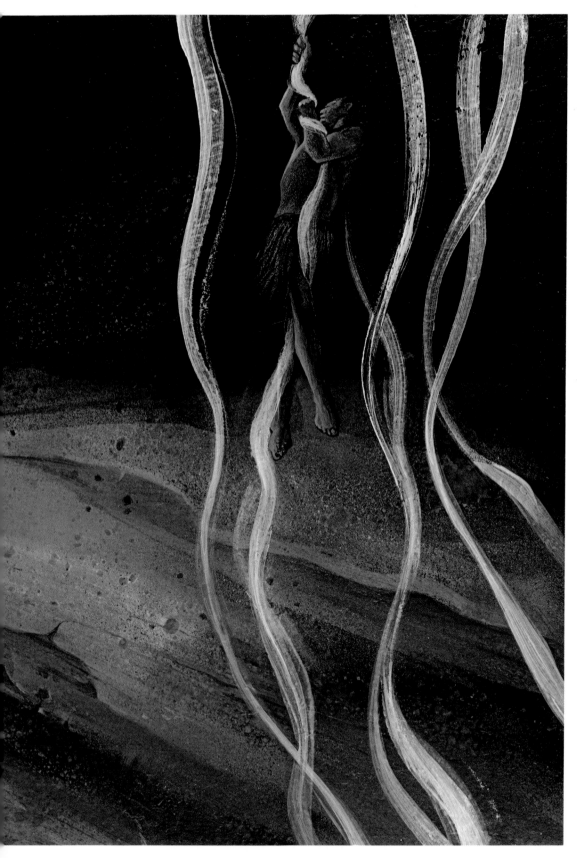

It is not clear how far Tane had to travel to reach the baskets and the stones in which the sacred knowledge was enshrined. One account says that he reached the tenth overworld where he engaged in purificatory rites. In the eleventh overworld he proceeded to Pu-motomoto, the gateway to the topmost heaven, where he was met by Rehua, the god of kindness, with whom he was well acquainted, and was presented with the coveted baskets.

In the meantime Whiro had been toiling slowly and painfully up the storeys of the sky. With his followers he lay in wait for Tane in the ninth heaven. A great battle ensued. The result was in doubt for some time but, strengthened by the knowledge he had gained in the ultimate overworld, Tane finally overcame Whiro and his hordes. They were driven down to earth where they made their permanent home. As a result mankind is constantly plagued by many of Whiro's followers.

Whiro himself was hurled headlong into the nether world where sickness, evil thoughts, and death are his gifts to men. He continues to father the Maiki-nui and Maiki-roa – the great and long-continuing misfortunes of mankind.

Tane, jubilant after his great accomplishment, left the overworld and entered the earthly whare kura, where he suspended the baskets with their precious freight from the rafters. The mana of the first of these stones, the Whatukura-a-Tangaroa, was subsequently conveyed to other stories in the many whare kura of Aotearoa, where they were used to seal the teaching of the tohunga, impressing the teaching on the minds of their pupils and adding mana to the recipients.

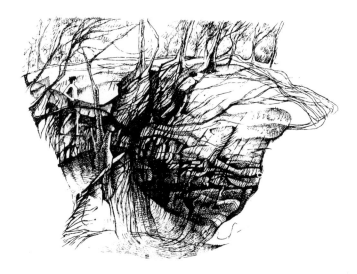

THE COMING OF LIFE

Although one of the youngest gods, Tane occupied an important place in the pantheon of deities. He was the life-giver, the fertiliser, the sustainer, the god of the forest and indeed of the whole world of nature, and the active element in all earthly life, as well as the bringer of knowledge. Among his descriptive names were Tane-mahuta, the source of trees, and Tane-mataahi, the creator of birds.

Apart from his feat in bringing the wananga to earth Tane's greatest accomplishment was his successful quest for the female element. The children of Papa and Rangi, the primal parents of earth and sky, were all male gods, instinct with the ira atua (divine element), and were incapable of producing the ira tangata (human element) which could only emerge from the uha (female element). In Tane's attempts to find the uha and create mortal life he bequeathed many gifts by which mankind has benefited. His mother Papa had advised him to visit Mumu-hango, an already existent female personification, and by mating with her he produced a variety of trees, birds, and insects. The union of Tane and other personifications resulted in a wide variety of natural phenomena such as stones, flood waters, muddy pools and monster reptiles. Two of their offspring in turn produced lizards, rocks, sandstone, gravel, and stone. But still a female element was missing.

After failing to achieve his purpose Tane returned to Papa who gave him the secret he needed. "Try the earth at Kurawaka," she said, "for in that place the female is in a state of virginity and potentiality. She is tapu, for she contains the seed of the likeness of man."

By this time Tane was in despair. "Old lady," he said, "there will never be any progeny for me." (This was surely the understatement of all time!)

"Go. Go to the Ocean who is grumbling there in the distance. When you reach the beach at Kurawaka gather up the earth in human form," Papa insisted.

Reluctantly Tane took her advice. On arrival at Kurawaka he fashioned an image of earth, to be the first woman, Hine-ahu-one, assisted by his brother gods. The older ones were responsible for shaping the body while the younger ones added the fat, muscles, and blood. Tane the fertiliser then lay on the new-formed body and put the breath of life into its mouth, nostrils, and ears. The eyelids opened, the eyes lit up, breath came from the nostrils, and the living body sneezed.

The mating of the first woman with a god resulted in the birth of a daughter, Hine-i-tauira. Later children of Hine-ahu-one included personifications of hot springs, clouds, and lightning.

The offspring of Tane and Hine-ahu-one were all girls. In spite of the fact that there are many different accounts of the creation of man it is doubtful whether such legends were ever part of the wananga, the teaching of the houses of learning. This in turn may account for the homely folktales that centre round the creation of Tiki, the first man. In one of them the progenitor is Tu-matauenga, the god of war, who represents upstanding man.

In one of the earliest accounts, the male element was of greater antiquity than the female, predating the separation of Rangi and Papa. Apparently a primitive form of vegetation was in existence prior to the separation, as well as an abundance of reddish water, and it was the combination of water and vegetation that is said to be responsible for the spontaneous generation of Tiki. His wife, Ma-rikoriko, originated by a more involved process. She was formed by A-rohirohi (mirage) and Pa-oro (echo). When their grand-daughter was born clouds floated in the sky, water flowed, and dry land rose above the floods. Earth could be seen in the first light of dawn, which turned to full day when Tane lifted Rangi from the embrace of Papa.

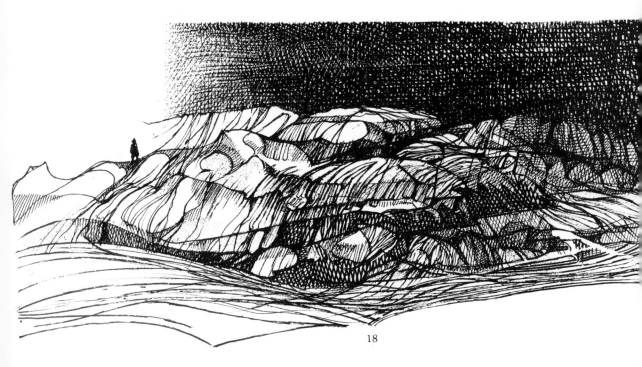

THE COMING OF DEATH

As Tane sowed the seeds of life in the Ao-marama, the world of light, so he was ultimately responsible for death, which comes sometimes with heart-rending sorrow, sometimes as a blessing, as during the sleep of the aged.

When his daughter Hine-i-tauira, or as she was so aptly named, Hine-titama (Girl of the Dawn) grew to womanhood, Tane took her to wife. When Hine-titama plied her husband with questions about her parents Tane was evasive and referred her to the posts of her mother's house which, he assured her, would reveal the identity of her father. The young woman was so persistent that at last Tane was forced to tell her the truth.

Saddened and disillusioned, Hine-titama determined to leave home.

"Where will you go?" Tane asked. "My presence is everywhere in this world of light. You cannot escape me."

"I shall not remain in your world of light," she said scornfully. "My grand-mother Papa will shelter me in the depths of her body. The path of Taheke-roa to the underworld shall be laid down for all time. From the Muri-wai-roa I shall look up to you and your offspring moving in the world."

Her final words were prophetic. "Remain, Tane, to pull up our offspring to day, while I go below to drag them down to night."

Tane protested, but Hine-titama was adamant. She chanted a sleep-inducing spell. Her parting gift to her father-husband was the Adam's apple which she placed in his throat as a token of their relationship. When quietness fell on the world of light, she descended through the space between the earth and the underworld. Ku-watawata, the guardian of the gates of the lower regions, attempted to dissuade her from going further but she remained firm, explaining that her purpose in going to the realms below was to protect her children of the upper world.

"Let me remain," she said, "that I may catch the living spirits of my descendants from the Ao-marama, the world of light."

When she took her place in the world of shadows her name was changed to Hine-nui-te-po – the great woman of night, or death. She became the goddess of death, but is also remembered as a young woman fleeing from her shame, yet imbued with love for her innocent offspring and their descendants. In the legend of Maui the demi-god and his attempted conquest of death, she is represented as the dread figure of night swallowing mankind but in the creation legends she is a pathetic and yet beneficent personage, devoted to the welfare of her children. It was not her wish, but the consequence of her incestuous relationship with Tane, that brought death into the world.

Although she was the first to tread the path to Rarohenga, the world beneath the world, she is there to welcome her children. The body of man perishes and decays, leaving its spirit free to go to Rarohenga, to the sunny girl of the dawn, who, through the evil that befell her, has become the last refuge of night and the mother of death. Tane remains as the protector of mortals in life, Hine-nui-te-po the guardian of their spirits in death.

The boundary between life and death is at Cape Reinga, the extreme north-western point of the North Island. Towards the point of departure came a never-ending procession of the spirits of the dead, or wairua. The far north must surely have been crowded with the ghostly, hurrying footsteps of people's souls. There are weird stories of parties of travellers who have been seen in the distance only to disappear as they came nearer and then to reappear behind the onlooker. The northern tribes were used to hearing the rustle and movement of countless unseen forms after a battle as the warriors who were killed made their final rendezvous in the world of light. It was said that chiefs could be distinguished from slaves. The rangatira passed to one side of a pataka (food store) while the slaves walked underneath. The kumara pits therefore faced north with their backs to the passing wairua lest they enter to make the contents tapu.

At the edge of the long, wind-swept beaches and hills the gales sometimes tied the flax leaves in knots, but according to those who lived there it was the work of the wairua. They left tokens of their passing – leaves of nikau, treeferns or bracken from those who came from inland parts, dune-grass or seaweed from coastal dwellers.

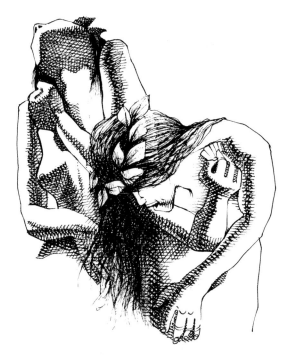

21

At the hill Taumata-i-haumu they paused and looked back at the land they had traversed. Here they wept and cut themselves with flakes of obsidian, plucked fresh leaves and wove kopare (mourning chaplets). The hills named Wai-hokimai and Wai-otioti were places for mourning and laceration. Here the wairua stripped off clothes made of wharangi, makuku and horopito leaves. They turned their backs on the world they had loved and, naked as at birth, prepared themselves for the final plunge at Te Reinga.

22

Some distance south of the Reinga they reached that notable stream Te Wai-ora-a-Tane, the life-giving waters of Tane – surely a sign that they were proceeding from an old to a new life. It was a spiritual Rubicon. Men and women who recovered from severe illness or wounds were said to have returned from the nearer bank of Te Wai-ora-a-Tane. Spirits that came from the east coast had to pass the perils of the Kapo-wairoa Stream at Tom Bowling Bay, where demons endeavoured to seize them as they crossed.

Having reached the rivers of no return on their northern journey, the wairua crossed the beach Te One-i-rehi (the Twilight Sands), ascended a slope, and passed over Te Wai-ngunguru (the Water of Lamentation), marching steadily forward to the end of the promontory and the gnarled old pohutukawa tree that overhung Te Reinga. It is to be noted that this term was applied not only to the entrance of the underworld but to the underworld itself, also known as Rarohenga.

The wairua waited until the waters swirled, displacing the surging bullkelp and revealing the entrance. They then climbed down the tree to leap into the clear water, into the underworld.

Although some emphasis has been placed on the nether regions as the final abode of the spirits – a belief that has its foundations in affection for Papa and the final embrace of the goddess of death – the Maori also shared the universal Polynesian teaching that the way of the soul led towards the setting sun.

After death the wairua lingered with the body for the length of time it takes a baby to be separated from its umbilical cord. At the end of its journey to the Reinga the wairua dived under the water and came to the surface at Ohau or Manawa-tahi in the Three Kings Islands. On the island a final hill remained to be climbed. Here the wairua chanted its farewell as it took its last glimpse of the world of light:

> *Ohau i waho ra e –*
> *E puke whakanutuinga*
> *Ohau in the distance –*
> *Last hill of farewell*

Thence the way stretched on to the sinking sun, the Ara-whanui-a-Tane (Path laid down by Tane), that leads to far Hawaiki, to Irihia, the Homeland.

Little is known of that mysterious abode to which the wairua go. Although some legends contradict each other, it was not necessarily a place of shadow and sorrow. There are several strange tales of living men and women who went to rescue loved ones from a premature death, though once food was eaten in the realm of Hine-nui-te-po there was no return. Of these tales, perhaps the legend of Hine-marama, her husband Rangi-rua and his brother Kaeo, is the most unusual.

Hine-marama died and her spirit went to the land of shadows. The heart-broken Rangi-rua enlisted the aid of his brother. Together they swung from the branches of the pohutukawa tree into the swirling waters that guard the entrance to Rarohenga. Emerging on dry land they followed the course of an underground stream until they saw a canoe coming to meet them from the far side. The evil-looking ferryman urged them to hurry but the brothers were afraid to enter his frail canoe lest it should sink under the weight of their mortal bodies. Kaeo solved the problem by swimming across the river.

It was not long before Rangi-rua found his wife and clasped her spirit to him. She looked at him sadly. "I cannot come with you," she replied to his urgent plea. "You are man and I am spirit. You must return quickly. Do not eat the food of this place or you will never be released."

"Have you eaten of it?" asked Rangi-rua.

"Not yet, my husband. There has not been time, for I have scarcely arrived. But see! The hangi is steaming and the food will soon be ready. Take Kaeo with you and lose no time in returning to the Ao-marama."

"You have not eaten!" Rangi-rua shouted. "Then we can save you!"

The brothers caught her hands and ran swiftly to the bank of the river. Husband and wife jumped into the canoe while Kaeo swam by their side.

"The woman stays here," the ferryman said curtly. "You are a man. You have no place here, Rangi. Go quickly while I return this woman to her proper place."

He caught her by the hand but Rangi-rua pulled her away and threw her on to the bank. Kaeo placed his foot against the prow of the canoe and sent it surging back into the stream.

On reaching her home the spirit of Hine said, "You must wash my body. Then I can return to it and be your wife again in this world of light."

And so it was. By the bravery of Rangi-rua and his brother Kaeo, Hine-marama was snatched from the clutches of Hine-nui-te-po, the goddess of death.

MAUI TAMES THE SUN

Maui-nukurau – The Deceiver
Maui-whare-kino – The Evil House
Maui-tinihanga – The Many Devices
Maui-i-toa – The Brave
Maui-i-atamai – The Kind
Maui-mohio – The Wise
Maui-mata-waru – The Eight Eyes, The Supernatural.

These were some of the descriptive names applied to the whimsical, irresponsible demi-god of Polynesia. After a miraculous birth and upbringing he won the affection of his parents, taught useful arts to mankind, snared the sun, tamed fire, discovered new lands by pulling them up from the bed of the sea, and eventually met his death while attempting to kill the goddess of death, Hine-nui-te-po. His malicious humour made his relatives highly suspicious of his motives, but his greatest deeds were of untold benefit to mankind – as when he snared and tamed the sun.

Te Ra, the sun, travelled swiftly across the sky. The hours of daylight were short. The nights were long and there was barely time to cook the morning and evening meal, no time to cultivate the plantation, to make war, to hunt, to fish, no time even to love.

"I'm going to capture the sun and force him to move more slowly!" Maui said to his brothers.

"Why?"

"It will make the days longer."

"Listen," they said earnestly, knowing how much trouble some of his experiments had caused. "No good can come of such foolishness. Leave the sun alone."

Maui laughed. "We shall do it together."

"We can never tame the sun," they protested. "He would burn us up before we could get near him."

"Not if you follow my plan," Maui said eagerly. "We'll plait strong ropes of flax. Early tomorrow morning we'll take them to where the sun rises. We can easily build shelters to shield us from the heat."

After some persuasion his brothers reluctantly set to work to plait ropes of flax fibre. As it was an unknown art, Maui had to teach them how to spin the fibre into flat, round, and square ropes with three and five strands.

It was a long journey, but at last they reached Te Rua-o-te-Ra, the Cave of the Sun. When he rose above the horizon a coil of rope fell over his head and shoulders, and another and another.

"Pull hard," Maui shouted. "Don't let him get away."

Leaving his brothers to maintain the strain on the ropes, he ran towards the sun. From his girdle he pulled out his favourite weapon, the jawbone of his ancestor Muri-ranga-whenua, and belaboured the helpless sun until he cried for mercy. Maui chanted a powerful spell, known as a punga, to keep the sun from moving.

"Are you trying to kill Tama-nui-te-ra?" said Tama in a weak voice, as he struggled to break the ropes. It was a significant remark, for it was the first time that the sacred name of the sun had ever been revealed.

"I have no wish to harm you. If you promise to travel more slowly in future, I'll let you go."

"No," said great Tama stubbornly. "Why should I change my habits on your account?"

"This is why," Maui said and battered the sun until he was weakened. When he was released he limped so slowly across the sky that men and women were able to cook their food, eat, work, play and make love at their leisure, while from his wounds came the bright rays we know as sunbeams.

After his long labour and the heat of the sun, Maui was thirsty. He called Tieke, the saddleback, to bring him a drink of water. The bird took no notice. Maui caught it in his hands and hurled it into the water. Where his hot hands touched Tieke's back the feathers were burned brown. He called Hihi, the stitch-bird, but it also ignored the demi-god. Maui threw it into a fire that tinged its plumage with yellow. Ever afterwards the stitchbird was nervous and timid. Toutouwai, the robin, was equally unco-operative and was marked with a patch of white at the root of its bill "as a mark of incivility". It was Kokako, the blue-wattled crow, who helped him. It flew to the water and brought back as much as it could carry in its ears. Maui rewarded it by pulling its legs so they were long and could move quickly.

There is another legend about Maui and the sun that refers to a period of perpetual daylight. The demi-god had become angered by the foolishness of mankind. They were so stupid that Maui felt the sunshine was being wasted on them. He held up his hand to stop the sunlight. It seems that he was unaware of the heat of the sun, for his hand was badly burnt. He rushed to the sea to assuage the pain and for the first time the sun set and darkness rushed across the land.

Maui rushed after the fleeing sun and dragged it back. It escaped and fled to the west. Maui pulled it back a second time and tied a long rope to it, attaching the other end to the moon.

When the sun set the moon was dragged above the horizon, giving light to the world by night as the sun had done by day.

Maui experimented more cautiously this time and found that he could hide the moon behind his hand without burning himself. Since then he has continued to use his hand to control the appearances of the moon.

A LEGEND OF THE MOON

Of the many legends of the heavenly bodies there is none more popular or wide-spread than the story of Rona, the woman in the moon.

She was loved by her husband but their lives were spoiled by her quick temper and the sharpness of her tongue.

There came a day when her husband said to her, "Tonight is one of the nights of the moon most favourable for fishing. I shall take the boys with me. We're going to the off-shore island where the fish are plentiful. We won't be back until tomorrow night. We should have a good catch by then. See that you have a good meal waiting for us."

The following day Rona prepared the oven and waited for her family to return home. When the shadows began to lengthen she lit the cooking fire. She had planned well, for as the heated stones glowed red in the dusk she heard the song of the returning fishermen. Before placing the food in the oven and covering it with greenery and earth, she discovered that she had no water to sprinkle over the hot stones.

The spring was at a little distance. Snatching up two calabashes she ran down the path. Darkness had fallen before she reached the spring, but a full moon was shining. The track showed up clearly in its silver light. Suddenly the moon was obscured by a passing cloud. Darkness rushed across the trees. She could not see her way and stubbed her toes on a projecting root. On trying to recover her balance she crashed into a rock and bruised her shin.

In her pain and exasperation she looked up and cursed the moon for having withdrawn its light.

"Pokokohua!" she shouted. "Cooked head!" – a malignant curse as well as an insult. The words were overheard by the moon, which descended from the sky and caught Rona in its hands and began to carry her away.

Rona caught at the branch of a ngaio tree and clung to it with all her might. Although her grasp of the tree could not be broken the roots were torn out of the ground and the woman was borne aloft, far into the sky, and placed on the surface of the moon. There she remains for all to see. With her are her calabashes and the ngaio tree which remained in her grasp during the violent journey.

It was a sad home-coming for her husband and children. The stones of the umu still glowed. The uncooked food still lay beside the oven, but there was no sign of Rona.

It was not until they looked up at the night sky that they realised that their hot-tempered wife and mother had angered the gods, for on the face of the full-bodied moon they saw her sitting disconsolate with her calabashes and the uprooted ngaio tree.

"Kia mahara ki te he o Rona," says the old proverb.
Remember the wrongful act of Rona.

TRIBAL GODS

When internecine warfare spread throughout Aotearoa, the various tribes could no longer claim the exclusive help of Tu-matauenga in their feuds. To the powerful departmental deities and other offspring of Rangi and Papa was added a number of tribal atua (gods). They were primarily war gods, though some had peaceful characteristics, being guardians of domestic and agricultural occupations. A few were regarded as more powerful than the others and on account of their prestige such atua were shared by a number of tribes. Prominent among such atua were those who had already won a reputation in Hawaiki and had been "imported" into Aotearoa, such as Maru, Uenuku, Rongo-mai, Kahu-kura, and Aitu-pawa. Others were "invented" to become the protagonists of their followers.

Each atua had an aria (manifestation). It is significant that many aria were natural phenomena. The rainbow, thunder and lightning, meteors, comets, and stars doubtless became associated with some important happening in tribal life and so were thought to be the manifestations of a particular god who looked favourably on his tribe or clan. They could then be depended upon to provide favourable or unfavourable omens for war parties, and for fishing and bird-hunting expeditions. Not infrequently the atua was in some fashion materialised in the person of a tohunga who interpreted his wishes and warnings. Maru and Uenuku may be taken to represent the more important tribal atua.

None was more widely known and venerated than Maru, a powerful war god noted, amongst other things, for the variety of canoes in which he was supposed to have been brought to Aotearoa. The Taranaki and Whanganui tribes claim that their forbears brought him with them in the *Aotea* canoe and that they offered the first bird taken in the forest to him instead of to Tane. The descendants of the *Arawa* say that he was brought by Kuiwai and Haungaroa, the sisters of the renowned tohunga Ngatoro-i-rangi, in the *Rewarewa* canoe, while others claim he made the voyage in the *Kurahaupo*. It has been conjectured that he was a voyager of great renown, one whose prowess brought such enduring fame that god-like powers were ascribed to him. His visible form is the red glow that is sometimes seen low on the horizon and is known as a maru. If it appeared in front of a taua or war party in an undeveloped state is was regarded as an evil omen. The taua would then cancel or postpone the expedition. If the maru was seen behind the war party in an arched form it was regarded as a favourable omen, and the attack would be launched with confidence.

On one notable occasion Maru, together with several companions, went down to the shore where they saw what appeared to be a dead whale lying on the sand, with gulls and flies swarming over it. The atua excavated a huge earth oven, heated the stones, and heaved the huge bulk into the pit.

Unfortunately for Maru and his friends the whale was not dead, and more important still, was not in fact a whale but an unusual form adopted by the even more powerful atua, Rongo-mai. The sleeping god awoke, reared its immense body in the air and crashed down on Maru and the atua who were assisting him. It is evident that this class of atua did not share the immortality of the primal gods for they were all killed. Maru himself, in the form he had adopted at the time, also succumbed – though not his essential spirit. Apparently it was only his material form or manifestation that had been destroyed, for Maru rose up to the overworlds and escaped Rongo-mai's wrath by hiding in a fissure in the rocks and from there he continued to influence the tribes who put their faith in him.

Uenuku was the most famous of the atua whose aria was the rainbow, one of his names being Uenuku-tawhana-i-te-rangi (Uneuku-bowlike-in-the-sky), and it is apparent that he was elevated, rather than born, to the status of a god. He was a famous ancestor in Hawaiki, the Homeland, and was deified in New Zealand.

It was in Aotearoa that his full name, Uenuku-tawhana-i-te-rangi, originated, for the reasons given in the following legend.

One morning, before it was light, Uenuku was wandering through the forest and after a time came in sight of a tiny lake he had not seen before. Two females who had descended from the sky were bathing there. One was Hine-pukohu-rangi, Girl of the Mist, and Hine-wai, the personification of light rain. After watching for some time Uenuku came to the bank and asked them where they lived.

"We are from Rangi-roa, from Rangi-mamao (the tall sky, the distant sky)," Hine-pukohu-rangi replied.

She turned abruptly to her sister, who was attracted to the handsome young man and seemed inclined to linger.

"Come," she said. "The full light of day is nearly here."

That night Uenuku sat beside the fire in his whare, his thoughts with Hine-pukohu-rangi. The flames died down to a dull glow and the door opened gently. The girl of his dreams stood in the doorway, waiting to be taken into his welcoming arms. They spent the night together and in the morning the young woman joined her sister and left for their home. Night after night Hine-pukohu-rangi returned to Uenuku's whare, but she warned him that he was not on any account to tell his friends of their liaison.

"The time will come, if you are patient," she told him. "When our baby is born you may reveal our relationship. By then I will be ready to live in your world of glaring light. But if you tell them before the baby comes I shall be forced to leave you."

It was difficult for Uenuku to keep silent. He was proud of his heaven-born wife and finally in an uncautious moment, he let fall a hint that was seized upon by the village gossips. They were sceptical and Uenuku was nettled. He soon persuaded himself that no harm could come from revealing the truth. If he was able to show his wife to the villagers then they would know that her beauty was above that of mortal women.

One night he carefully blocked up all the crevices in the walls of the whare to ensure that no light could penetrate the gloom.

At the usual time of waking Hine stirred. "The night is over," she murmured. "I must leave."

"It is still dark. Go back to sleep," Uenuku replied.

Much later she stirred restlessly. "It is a long night," she said. "Are you sure that daylight is not near?"

"Yes, the night must be over," Uenuku said. He opened the door. Sunlight flooded the whare.

Hine-pukohu-rangi uttered a cry of distress. She rushed outside, stopped and looked reproachfully at her husband. Uenuku was standing by the door with pride in his bearing, as his friends gathered round in a semi-circle uttering exclamations of surprise and approval.

"I did not think you would betray me," she said sadly. She went inside the whare again. Standing under the smoke vent she murmured, "Uenuku! You have shamed me when the morning star appeared and the sun arose. The cry of Hine-wai had not reached me as we lay inside the house. Now I am indeed ashamed in the sight of all your people."

Once again she went through the doorway and rose swiftly to the gable. Uenuku tried to grasp her, but she evaded him. Mist swirled round and hid her from his sight. Like two gauzy clouds Hine-pukohu-rangi and Hine-wai rose into the sky and were never seen again.

In spite of his imprudence Uenuku was deeply in love with his wife and he set out in search of her. Year after year was spent in a vain quest, for he never found the wife of his youth. He grew old and, in a distant country, death at last overtook him. Then the gods took pity on him. They set him in the sky where he became the rainbow that spans the heaven and the atua of fighting men.

In one version of the legend Hine-pukohu-rangi returned temporarily to her home after the birth of her child, named Heheu-rangi, and sang a lament for the child whom she was forced to leave in the world in which she could no longer remain.

There is symbolic significance in the story. Heheu-rangi is the Sky-clearer. Hine-pukohu-rangi's aria can be seen in the rising mist. Hine-wai is the personification of misty rain, and Uenuku the atua who personifies the rainbow.

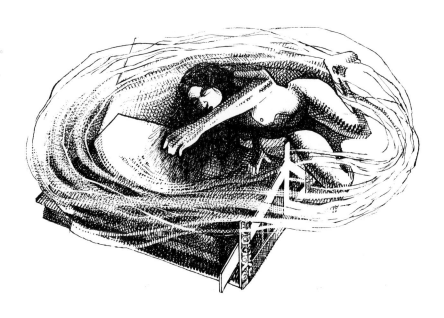

THE COMING
OF KUMARA

In view of the widespread cultivation of the succulent tuber known to the Maori as kumara, in the North Island and in the more sheltered districts of the South Island, it is not surprising that a variety of myths was invented to explain its origin.

The kumara was imported to New Zealand, which fact in turn necessitated a further series of legends to account for its arrival in the southern islands. There are several versions of the manner in which it was brought, one of them concerning Pou-rangahua who lived near the mouth of the Waipaoa River in the days when men lived on the products of lake, river, sea, and forest. It was the craving of Pou's baby son for a mysterious, unknown food that sent the chief far across the Ocean of Kiwa, which we now call the Pacific, to try to satisfy his child's demands.

At Pari-nui-te-ra his quest succeeded, for there was the site of a famous kumara plantation; but on landing his canoe was wrecked and he had no means of returning to his home. He was compensated for his loss by winning the friendship of the chief Tane, who not only supplied him with an abundant supply of kumara but was also prepared to lend him one of his pet birds, feathered monsters so large and powerful that they were able to carry a grown man on their backs. Pou-rangahua slung two baskets of kumara across the shoulders of one of the birds. It ran quickly along the sand, but under the double load was unable to lift itself from the beach. Tane promptly led forth his favourite bird, the largest and strongest of all, and on its strong back Pou, with the baskets, at last began his flight back to Aotearoa. Skilfully avoiding all the perils of the journey, he arrived safely back at his home.

And so, according to the ancient legend, the kumara came to Aotearoa, the gift from Hawaiki that revolutionised the diet of the Polynesians in this far-off land. But Pou-rangahua failed to heed the instructions of his generous host. Though he had been careful to avoid the clutches of Tama-i-waho, the ogre of Hikurangi, on his homeward journey, he was culpably careless of the welfare of Tane's bird when he sent it back to its master.

"Pou returns," he said, "and closes the door for ever."

At Pari-nui-te-ra the Polynesian chief waited in vain for the bird he loved. But tired after its long flight and then exhausted by the further flight that Pou had demanded from landfall to home, it had fallen victim to the ogre of Hikurangi.

Roger Hardly

Other legends relate to a mythical origin, which influenced the elaborate ritual surrounding its cultivation and harvesting. Pani, or Pani-tinaku as she is sometimes known, was the "mother" or personification of the kumara. She was the wife of Rongo-maui, a brother of Whanui; when the star Whanui rose above the horizon, the time had come, said the wise old tohunga, to lift the crop.

Many are the tales that are told of how Pani gave birth to the kumara, tales of how the precious food was stolen from the gods by Rongo-maui and given to the sons of men. It was a heinous theft that robbed the atua of their food and, indeed, it was regarded as the origin of all theft. Whanui looked down at the men and women toiling like ants in their cultivations and in anger sent Anuhe, Toronu, and Moka to destroy the stolen fruits of the earth. It was so then and is still today, for these are the different kinds of caterpillar that feed on the foliage of the tubers.

According to a legend preserved by the tribes of Tuhoe, Pani cared for the five Maui brothers after the death of their parents. One day, when they returned from fishing, they complained to Rongo-maui that he was lazy because he never accompanied them on their fishing expeditions, and failed to help supply the family with food. Rongo resented the criticism. He made up his mind to give them a food supply that would prove he was a better provider than the foster-children of his wife. It was then that he climbed up to the realm of the gods and stole the essence of their food. Descending to earth he impregnated his wife with the seed, the life-spirit of the kumara. When her time came, Rongo told her to go to the stream of Mona-ariki to give birth. As she stood in the sacred water she produced her young, the children who were named Nehutai, Patea, Pio, Matatu, Pauarangi, and several others. These are the names of the varieties of kumara provided by that ancestor as food for her descendants.

Then the sacred ovens were prepared, and so men learned the art of cooking food. Had it not been for Rongo-maui, men would be like birds and lizards that eat their food raw.

More than one canoe lays claim to the honour of introducing the kumara to Aotearoa; but it is to Pani-tinaku and her husband Rongo-maui that we render homage for providing mankind with the food of the gods, and to Whanui, the star whose appearance reminds men it is time to harvest the fruits of their labour.

SYMBOL OF FERTILITY

The mauri, the supernatural force that guarded the food supplies of a forest, eel weir, or plantation was jealously guarded. It frequently resided in a stone.

In the forests of Pukekohe the mauri was kept in a secret place on a hillside, its location known only to the ariki of the tribe. The forests were well stocked with such birds as the kereru, tui, and kaka, and the streams were replete with tuna – eels. The fame of the Pukekohe mauri had spread as far as the Urewera and there a young rangatira of Tuhoe offered to obtain the mauri and bring it to his people, where it would doubtless increase the fertility of the forests of the Urewera.

He left his home burdened with feathered ornamental cloaks and greenstone ornaments. After a long journey he was made welcome at the large kainga at Pukekohe where, on account of his appearance and ostentatious display of wealth, he attracted the attention of a young woman of high lineage. He courted her assiduously, won her affections, and settled down as a member of his wife's tribe.

The ariki spoke to him one day. He spread his fingers far apart and said, "If you climb the hill over there, and hold up your hand with your fingers wide apart, the kereru will fly down and put their heads between them."

The man of Tuhoe expressed incredulity. The ariki was offended. To maintain the honour of his tribe he offered to demonstrate the power of the mauri on condition that his confidence would not be misplaced.

The two men entered the forest and, as they climbed the hill, they could see the kereru perched on every tree, feeding on the berry-laden branches. When they approached the mauri, the kereru flew down from the trees and put their heads between the chief's fingers.

The young man was still sceptical. "Your mana is greater than mine," he admitted, "but that is no proof that your forests yield more than those of my tribe or any other I have seen."

The ariki was startled by the obtuseness of the young man, for whom he had some admiration.

"You may have travelled far," he said, "but you have little knowledge. There can be no doubt that the richness of our land is above that of any tribe, nor that any other possesses a mauri of such power."

The Tuhoe rangatira expressed surprise. "You have certainly benefited by the natural richness of land and water, the fame of which I heard even in my home, but unless I see the mauri for myself, and feel its power, whether stick or stone, I certainly cannot believe in it."

The exasperated ariki led the rangatira to an ancient rata tree. In a hollow beneath the trunk lay a round stone. The ariki would not permit him to touch it but even at a distance the young man could sense an aura of tremendous power. Obviously the stone was not light, but it could be carried by a man in one hand.

In the months that followed he kept his promise of secrecy. He told no one of the ariki's indiscretion in showing him the hiding place of the mauri, but his purpose in taking it to his own people was not forgotten.

When the season for replenishing the pataka arrived he took no part in bird-hunting expeditions but joined the eeling parties, often staying out all night, returning late in the morning in order that the people should become accustomed to his being away from home.

One evening he set out early on the pretence of catching eels. He left the cloaks and greenstone ornaments behind as a gift to his wife and those who had befriended him. Lifting the mauri gently from its resting place, he stowed it in the eel basket, and made his way out of the forest.

At daybreak the bird-spearers left the kainga. When they entered the forest they were surprised at the quiet that invaded it. There were no movements in

the tree tops, no bird sounds. The silence was oppressive. They summoned the ariki who at once suspected what had happened. He ran to the rata and peered into the hole. As he feared, the mauri was missing.

He summoned a meeting of the kaumatua. No one could offer an explanation until it was reported that the stranger from Tuhoe had set out alone the previous evening and had not returned. There could be no doubt that the ariki's confidence had been misplaced, and that the young rangatira had stolen their mauri.

Two taua were soon on his trail, one travelling on the Waikato River by canoe, the other marching overland. They could detect no sign, however, of the passing of the fugitive who had gone up-river in a small fishing canoe, abandoning it at Taupiri. He had then crossed the swamps to reach the Maungatautari Range.

The stone in his eel bag seemed to grow heavier with every step he took. Looking back from the crest of a hill that had taken toll of his strength he saw his pursuers climbing steadily towards him. They had picked up his trail on leaving the swamps and, lacking his heavy burden, were gaining rapidly.

Picking up the basket he had placed on the ground he ran as quickly as he could, heading for Rotorua where he hoped to find shelter. Yet even as the thought of rescue by hereditary enemies of the Pukekohe people entered his mind he realised it was hopeless to try and reach the distant Arawa pa. Already he could hear the thud of feet on the ground and the sound of bodies crashing through the undergrowth. In front of him there was a small lake. Knowing there was no hope of eluding his pursuers, nor of taking the mauri to his own people, he determined that no one else might benefit from the stone and so threw himself over a bluff and sank to the bottom of the lake with the mauri clasped firmly in his arms.

Neither the rangatira of Tuhoe nor the mauri of Pukekohe was ever seen again. The men of the taua returned sadly to their home. As they entered the forest that surrounded the kainga they could see that some of the birds had returned, but they were few in number. The sacred talisman that had attracted them and kept them within the compass of its influence was no longer there

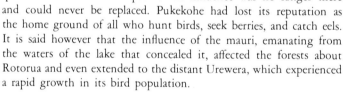

and could never be replaced. Pukekohe had lost its reputation as the home ground of all who hunt birds, seek berries, and catch eels. It is said however that the influence of the mauri, emanating from the waters of the lake that concealed it, affected the forests about Rotorua and even extended to the distant Urewera, which experienced a rapid growth in its bird population.

ENCHANTMENT

In addition to personifications and local atua, the landscape was always liable to invasion by tipua, usually regarded as demons or goblins. The term was frequently used in an adjectival sense and can best be translated as "enchanted". A rakau tipua, for instance, was an enchanted log. Birds, fish, dogs, stones, lakes, mountains, rivers and other objects, animate or inanimate, could under certain circumstances become tipua.

Ordinary objects could suffer enchantment and be imbued with unearthly qualities. Some became tipua in a manner that was beyond earthly control; in other cases the enchantment was a result of deliberate action. If the body of a deceased person of some importance was placed at the foot of a tree while the bearer rested, the wairua, or part of its essence, would attach itself to the tree which would then become tipua. Depositing the umbilical cord of a new-born child would have the same effect on a tree or a boulder.

Tipua objects were not tapu nor were they worshipped. They were simply enchanted, and therefore possessed strange powers. The tipua needed to be placated by offerings of twigs, sprays, or branches of a living tree. Leaves of the karamu or kawakawa were favoured not only to protect the traveller but also to increase the mana of the tipua. The custom of depositing green offerings was known as uruuruwhenua. The offering was invariably made when the tipua object was first passed and customarily on every subsequent occasion, the surrounding bush often being denuded of foliage.

One notable object to which the offering was made is the stone that sheltered the Rotorua notability Hatupatu when he was pursued by Kurangaituku, the bird-woman. The large boulder by the roadside is a familiar sight to travellers.

Floating logs frequently possessed mysterious powers. Such a log was of great assistance to a young woman who lived on the foothills of the Huiarau Range. Hinerau was famed for her beauty and was courted by young men of noble birth from the surrounding villages. She was gracious to all her suitors but had not found one to whom she could give her heart.

Conscious of her beauty she dressed her hair with care and carried a sachet of sweet-scented moss. The aromatic plants were not easily found and, on one occasion, her search took her far from her home. She lost her way and came unexpectedly to Lake Waikaremoana. Hoping to meet someone who could direct her to her kainga she wandered along the shore. Suddenly the land was shaken by a violent earthquake. The shore was lifted and the lake receded. Where there had been gently sloping forest land tall cliffs now rose abruptly. The water rushed back, swirling round her, and ebbed again. There was a roar of threshing trees and rumbling landslides, then silence. The ground ceased its movement and Hinerau found that she was confined to a narrow strip of gravel. On every side deep water lapped against the newly formed cliff face; she was imprisoned on a shelf of rock and gravel.

She lay on the barren shelf throughout the night, shivering with cold and loneliness. When the moon rose she took a sharp-edged shell and scratched

through the fibre of a flax leaf until it was severed, then made some marks on it, hoping they would be recognised by one of her lovers who might by this time be searching for her.

Murmuring a prayer to the atua she threw the leaf into the water. Almost immediately she heard unearthly music and in the bright path of moonlight on the lake a rakau tipua drifted toward her. It swept past, caught the flax leaf in its projecting branches, and disappeared into the distance. The music died away. Hinerau's tears dripped on to the rocks and formed a rivulet that grew into a rushing torrent, later known as Te Tangi-o-Hinerau (The Weeping of Hinerau).

Day turned to night and night to day as she sat alone. Suffering hunger she prayed to Rehua for help, and the god of kindness heard her request and sent a flock of kaka. As they circled round she caught one or two of them. Recalling how bird hunters killed them by biting their necks, she also tried to do so, but in spite of her hunger did not have the heart to treat the birds in this way.

Meanwhile the enchanted log had drifted to the other side of the lake. It grounded near the home of the young chief Te Toru, the flax leaf waving like a banner on a branch of the log. The leaf fell into the water and floated to the feet of the chief. Then, to the sound of the weird music, the log went on its way. Te Toru picked up the leaf and in some way was able to construe its message. He launched a small canoe and paddled to the other side of the lake, where he found Hinerau and rescued her.

He took her to wife and she bore him many sons while the wandering log gathered fame as the tipua of Waikaremoana. It seems likely that it was the famous singing log Tutaua that was known to several generations. It had first been placed there by Hau-mapuhia, who formed the lake, and who may herself have been tipua, though she is usually described as a taniwha. The Tuhoe people had a saying they used when they heard its music – Ko Tutaua e waiata haere ana (It is Tutaua singing as it goes).

The log occasionally drifted ashore. In the course of time it grew malevolent. Whoever touched it was stranded as Hinerau had been, or suffered misfortune in some other way. Finally it disappeared through the outlet at Te Wharawhara, doubtless to the relief of the Tuhoe people. In later years one member of the tribe said, "I myself heard Tutaua, the log demon, singing far out upon the waters, singing in a strange voice like the whistling of the wind."

PATUPAIAREHE

Pleasant in its sun-dappled freshness, and in the cool depths where the sun seldom penetrated, prolific as a store house of bird life, the bush could in places harbour malevolent creatures that went by names such as patupaiarehe and maero. The latter were the wild men of the forest, ever ready to pounce on unwary travellers. They were found more frequently in the rain forests of the South Island than in the sunnier North Island bush.

The patupaiarehe are usually described as fairies in English, but this description is misleading if we think of fairies as dimunitive and lovable "little people". The patupaiarehe were usually described as being taller than humans, fair-skinned, red-haired and dangerous to mortals. They were found in several parts of the North Island, but were most numerous in certain localities such as Ngongotaha, Pirongia and Moehau, where they were supposed to inhabit large fortified villages on the gloomy, mist-frequented heights of the mountains.

It has been suggested that they were a racial memory of fair-skinned people of distant countries. Another theory is that the earliest immigrants to Aotearoa, dispossessed of their lands by late arrivals, took refuge in the bush, building pa on the cloudy summits of the hills and descending from time to time in the concealing mist to abduct and ravish young women. The theory is supported by the belief that diggers of fern-root sometimes heard a mysterious voice that said, "You rejoice today, but my turn will come tomorrow." When the fernroot diggers heard it they set aside the first three roots as an offering to the original inhabitants of the land. Yet another belief was that wairua who had failed to reach the land of spirits were condemned to haunt the forest and hide themselves from the bright light of day. In this respect they had some affinity with kehua, the ghosts who emerged at night to terrify anyone rash enough to venture into the darkness. There is a legend that relates their arrival in the *Tainui* canoe; another that says they were placed in their mountain retreats by the tohunga Ngatoro-i-rangi who came in the *Arawa* canoe. Again it has been said that some patupaiarehe are descended from the atua Tama-o-hoi who divided Ruawahia from Tarawera (see pages 91–2).

The various branches of the patupaiarehe had certain features and habits in common, though differing in other respects. The urukehu among the Maori, being light-haired with fair skin, were often regarded as descendants of the patupaiarehe through mixed marriages with mortal women. To a darker-skinned people, the untattooed white-skinned beings were regarded as supernatural. They lived in pa made of the vines of the kareao (supplejack) and ventured far from their pa only on wet or misty days. The plaintive notes of their koauau and putorino exercised a fatal fascination on young women who were lured to the homes of the patupaiarehe. Those who were abducted seldom returned, but lived in a permanently dazed condition amongst their captors.

Fortunately there were two methods of defence against the iwi atua, the supernatural tribe – cooked food and red ochre, which was freely used on tapu objects. The use of these deterrents is illustrated in the following two legends, from Ngongotaha and Pirongia.

Ruarangi and his young wife lived in the foothills of the Hakarimata Range. Tawhaitu was gathering kumara tubers when her neck was encircled by a strong white arm. She was swept off her feet and carried into the forest. Wet leaves brushed against her. The mist trailed damp fingers over her face. At the summit of Pirongia the patupaiarehe laid Tawhaitu gently on a bed of moss in one of the whare of the ghostly pa. She lay in his arms throughout the long night listening to the plaintive music of the fairy people and the thin wailing of koauau and putorino while Whanawhana, her abductor and the chief of the hapu, told her of his love. Towards morning she fell into a karakia-induced sleep.

When she woke she found herself lying in a forest clearing near her own home. Her husband Ruarangi was kneeling beside her, looking at her with an anxious expression. He had spent the night searching for her. Hiding her face in his breast she told him how she had been ravished by the dreaded patupaiarehe.

"Whanawhana has laid his evil spell on me," she sobbed. "When it is dark again I shall be drawn to him. I know he has taken my will. I shall not be able to resist his power."

In his distress Ruarangi consulted the tohunga. "There are ways to overcome the patupaiarehe," the tohunga advised him. "You must build a small wharau. Lay a heavy beam across the threshold and paint it with kokowai (red ochre). You must also smear the kokowai over your bodies and your garments.

"When this is done, dig a hole for an umu, light the fire, place food in it, and cover it well. If you do this in the late afternoon the smell of cooking food will last all night and protect your wife as she lies in the wharau."

That night the slowly steaming umu wafted a savoury smell round the wharau, guarding Ruarangi and Tawhaitu from Whanawhana. Outside the hut stood the tohunga, naked, chanting karakia to repel the patupaiarehe.

Whanawhana and three companions appeared before the wharau. When they attempted to enter they were driven back by the priest's incantations and the smell of cooking food, nor would they have dared to step over the painted beam laid across the doorway. Step by step they retreated slowly to the forest.

Tuwhaitu was not troubled again, although her union with Whanawhana proved fruitful and their descendants, who live by the Waipa River, are noted for the reddish tinge in their hair.

The best known of the fairy legends comes from the experiences of Ihenga, the great explorer and name-giver of the thermal region. In the course of his journeys he came to Rotorua – Roto-rua-a-Ihenga, the second lake of Ihenga. Travelling around the shore, he reached the stream and mountain which we now know as Ngongotaha.

Ihenga was curious to know whether the plume that drifted lazily from the hilltop was smoke or mist. He climbed the slopes, undaunted by the plaintive songs he heard in the forest. From the corner of his eye he saw strange forms, and movements that showed he was being followed.

A breath of wind tore the mist away from the peak, revealing the palisades of a pa and a tree blazing like a torch. He broke off a branch that was alive with flame. Pale forms rushed towards him. Ihenga swung the crackling branch in a fiery circle that caused the patupaiarehe to retreat. He plunged it into the bracken, filling the air with choking smoke and stinging sparks and fled back to his canoe.

Some time later he settled by the Waiteti Stream and tried to establish relations with the elusive white-skinned people whose music echoed eerily through the mist. One day he climbed up to the hilltop pa and called to the red-haired people of the mist. They ran towards him. He asked for water and a beautiful young woman offered him a drink from a calabash with a wooden mouthpiece. Ihenga drank deeply while the patupaiarehe crowded around and commented on his appearance. Ihenga named the mountain from this incident. Ngongo means "to drink" and is also the word for the mouthpiece of a taha, or calabash.

The strange inhabitants or Te Tuahu-a-te-atua, the sacred place of the god, plied him with questions and touched his body with ghostly fingers. Ihenga grew afraid. He slipped through the palisades and hurtled down the hillside.

The patupaiarehe streamed after him. Gradually he drew away from the shouting throng, but one of the fairy creatures kept close on his heels. It was the young woman who had offered him her calabash. She threw her garments away to leave her limbs unhampered. Ihenga knew that if she captured him she would rob him of his memory, and he would never see his wife again.

In the pocket of his belt there was a small fragment of kokowai mixed with shark oil. Without faltering in his headlong flight he drew it out and smeared it over his body, for he remembered that the patupaiarehe were repelled by kokowai and that the smell of food and oil was repugnant to them.

With a cry that had sadness and longing in it as well as frustration, the comely girl from the fairy pa stood still. Ihenga looked back and saw her motionless amongst the trees with arms stretched out in mute appeal to the mortal man who had escaped her clutches.

The experience of Ruru, the husband of Tangi-roa, was more painful. While on a tuna-catching expedition, the young man was lost in the hills. Presently he stumbled into a clearing and was immediately surrounded by white, ghostly forms that caught him and carried him away to their pa. For a long time he was kept in the strange comatose state of most captives of the patupaiarehe.

Attractive young women were usually loved and cared for by the male fairies, but Ruru was subjected to many indignities. They rubbed him with the palms of their hands and the soles of their feet until a strange moss or lichen began to grow from his skin and covered his body. The hair on his head fell out and he became completely bald.

After a time he was granted partial liberty. He was allowed to roam through the forest to search for berries and hunt for eels and birds; but as the patupaiarehe were unable to use fire in their damp retreat, the food was unpalatable.

Thinking that Ruru was dead, the aged tohunga Maringi-rangi sought to marry Tangi-roa, but was supplanted by a younger rival. The tohunga went to the seashore and wove spells of peculiar intensity, after which he lay down to sleep. When he woke he found a stranger sitting beside him. Maringi-rangi looked at him closely. The man was naked and covered with a peculiar moss-like growth in which the bald crown of his head lay like a polished boulder. The tohunga looked at him closely for a long time and then said, "You are Ruru! It is because of my magic that you have escaped from the patupaiarehe. Come with me."

He led Ruru along the beach and through the gates of the kainga. A cry of horror rose from the women, who shouted, "A madman!"

"Don't be afraid," Maringi-rangi said. "This is our old companion Ruru. Call Tangi-roa. Tell her that her husband has come to claim her once again as his wife."

Tangi-roa ran towards them, but recoiled when she saw the bald-pated, lichen-covered travesty of a man. Maringi-rangi led Ruru up to her and said with an evil smile, "Here is your reward, Tangi-roa. Welcome your lover and husband." The woman buried her face in her hands and wept bitterly. Looking down at her, the old tohunga's heart was touched. He remembered the passions and sorrows of his youth.

"Bring warm water quickly," he ordered.

Dipping his hands in the calabash, he repeated spells and incantations and rubbed the body of Ruru as the patupaiarehe had done when they had captured the young man. The kohukohu, or moss, came away freely and Ruru was restored to his wife — but to his dying day his skull remained as smooth as a water-worn boulder in the stream where he had hunted for tuna before he was caught by the fairy folk of the hills.

THE RESTLESS MOUNTAINS

In the year 1864 Te Kani-a-takirau, the most powerful chief of the east coast, was proposed as Maori King. The offer was made by Te Heuheu of Taupo. Te Kani refused the invitation, saying that he was born a king and could not have kingship conferred on him.

Te Heuheu replied, "You may be king of the east coast, but I want you to be king of all the Maori people of Aotearoa and stamp out the mana of that woman queen."

"My kingdom is like my mountain Hikurangi," Te Kani said proudly. "It is inherited and permanent and not like your Tongariro, a wanderer."

The metaphor referred to the legend of the wandering mountains of the volcanic plateau, of which there are many versions.

In the long ago many mountains lived together in the centre of the North Island. Tongariro, not then truncated, but rearing his snow-clad form far into the clouds, was the ariki. Near him stood Taranaki (Mount Egmont), Tauhara and Putauaki. They were all proud and valiant warriors. The only woman among them was Pihanga, rounded in soft curves, clad in a cloak of green foliage.

The male mountains all coveted this gentle female mountain and fought fiercely for her love. Tongariro was the victor. He wrapped her in soft arms of cloud, and drove the other mountains far away. They departed at night and hastily, for they knew that their progress would be arrested by the rising sun.

Tauhara and Putauaki journeyed towards the sea. Tauhara was the tardy one, often looking backwards, and progressed no further than the northern shore of Lake Taupo. Putauaki travelled to the end of the Kaingaroa Plain and, as Mount Edgecumbe, stands as the sentinel of the Bay of Plenty.

Taranaki, mightier than Tauhara and Putauaki, said, "Ka haere au ki te towene-tanga o te ra" – "I shall go to the setting place of the sun." As he travelled away he ploughed a mighty furrow, down which the Wanganui river flows, and took up a position on the western tip of the island, where he still hurls taunts at the victorious Tongariro.

TANIWHA

The folklore of Aotearoa is replete with tales of grisly monsters that inhabited dark caves and deep pools – a menace to travellers who were unaware of their presence. Monstrous in size as well as form, they were called taniwha. Although most were notorious man-eaters, many could be placated by gifts of food and the reciting of karakia and others were believed to be harmless except when tormented or neglected. The ocean-dwelling taniwha were known to have rescued ship-wrecked parties, escorted sea-going canoes and even carried men on their backs. Such creatures were sometimes in the shape of sharks, sometimes whales.

More usually they were huge reptiles in form, with an insatiable desire for human flesh, even for whole canoe-loads of people. Interestingly there were no reptiles in Polynesia that could have given rise to the concept of crocodile-like monsters, and this has led to the speculation that they were a racial memory from tropical lands. Taniwha frequently resembled lizards (and were called by the same name – moko), of which the Maori had a superstitious fear, believing them to be the living representation of the powers that caused sickness and death.

Taniwha had a distinguished ancestry, having descended from the union of the great god Tane and Hine-tupari-maunga. Their daughter Putoto married Tane's brother Taka-aho and gave birth to Tua-rangaranga, the progenitor of taniwha. Others, not in this direct line of descent, were believed to be ancestors; where taniwha had originally been human beings, or were inhabited by their wairua, they shared the immortality of the wairua.

Their habitat could vary. They frequently dwelt in water – salt or fresh – but some lived on land or could even fly. There were notable occasions when they lived and travelled underground and engaged in the earth-moving business, making considerable changes in the landscape.

From the thermal regions come the following three stories of taniwha.

Many travellers between Rotorua and Taupo had failed to reach their destination. It was suspected that they had been ambushed by some hostile tribe. A taua was sent out to find the enemy and destroy them. As the party travelled across the plain the scent of the men crept into the nostrils of Hotu-puku, who was lurking in a nearby cave.

The monster sprang out and rushed towards the unsuspecting men. The spines and excrescences on its back had the appearance of growths on some fabulous creature of the sea. Some of the men were trampled to death, others were seized

in the cavernous mouth and swallowed whole. Those who escaped stumbled into the pa at Rotorua and told the tale of their misadventures.

Another war party was quickly assembled and took the trail to Hotu-puku's lair.

On the way they discussed their plan of campaign. On arrival at Kapenga, where the taniwha still lurked, they stripped leaves from ti-palms and plaited them into strong ropes.

They waited until the wind blew away from the cave and climbed down to it. They could hear the monster's stertorous breathing. It was sleeping soundly. The rope snares were arranged at some distance from the cave while the men drew close to the entrance. They were armed with cutting and thrusting weapons. Others held the ropes while a third party, composed of the youngest and boldest of the warriors, stood at the mouth of the cave to lure the taniwha into the open. They advanced cautiously as the ground shook and the huge form of Hotu-puku filled the dark mouth of the cave. It came forward at a run, its jaws distended, its long tongue darting from side to side. As the taniwha rushed out, the warriors retreated. Their ropes were lying on the ground, seemingly scattered at random, but in fact they had been placed with great care. The men took care not to disturb them.

A sudden shout startled the taniwha. The noose sprang from the ground as a score of hands tugged at the ropes. Hotu-puku's front legs were caught in a crushing grip. Like living things the other ropes circled its legs and body. They wove themselves round its neck and jaws, falling lightly and then biting into the scaly flesh. Only the tail was free. It lashed from side to side, sweeping men off their feet as the monster felt the bite of mere and taiaha, and the sting of cutting implements.

Maddened with pain, Hotu-puku strained against the ropes as the nooses were pulled tighter. The ropes were wound round the trunks of trees, pegging the taniwha down firmly until it lay lifeless on the ground.

Its appearance was that of a huhu grub, if one can imagine such an object swollen to the size of a young whale, or of a giant tuatete or tuatara, with scales and spiny ridges.

One of the chiefs suggested that they throw off their garments and cut the monster open to inspect the contents of its belly. There were many layers of fat to penetrate, but once these were stripped off the excited warriors exposed a grisly treasure trove. There were bodies of men and women who had recently been eaten and were still undigested. There were many greenstone mere, weapons such as kokiri and taiaha, weapons made from the bones of whales, sharks' teeth, mats, garments of dogs' hair, cloaks ornamented with albatross, kiwi, and kaka feathers, garments of dressed and undressed flax, and precious heirlooms.

The human remains were interred, after which the taniwha was dismembered and oil expressed from its fat. It was eaten by the warriors to express their contempt and to celebrate victory over the enemy that had killed so many of their friends from Rotorua and Taupo-moana.

One of the more well-disposed taniwha was Horomatangi. He had been brought from Hawaiki by the famous tohunga Ngatoro-i-rangi. After Ngatoro's arrival in Aotearoa his sister Kuiwai was grievously insulted in the homeland by her husband. Together with her sister Haungaroa she came to the new land across the sea in search of Ngatoro to ask him to avenge the insult. The tohunga was unaware of their arrival but the watchful Horomatangi, who at that time was in the vicinity of White Island, saw them.

He then swam under the water until he reached the mainland, travelled underground, and came to the surface of Lake Taupo where he blew a column of water and pumice high into the air, creating a whirlpool some three or four kilometres south of Motutaiko at the Horomatangi Reef. From the lake he saw Kuiwai and Haungaroa in the distance. For some reason the taniwha was unable to reach the women and was forced to communicate with them by signs. Turning and twisting, Horomatangi travelled underground again. At Wairakei he exhaled violently. The earth shuddered as the steam of his breath broke through the ground, forming the Karapiti blow-hole. The white plume of condensing breath gushed high into the air and turned towards Ngatoro's resting place at Maketu. Kuiwai saw the column of steam and interpreted the taniwha's sign correctly.

Exhausted by his labours, Horomatangi remained in the channel between Motu-taiko, the little island at the southern end of Lake Taupo, and Wairakei, where he was transformed into a black rock. He sometimes assumes the form of a lizard and is then known as Ihumataotao.

On the nearby promontory of Motutere there once stood an extensive pa, and a church erected more than a hundred years ago. The church had a short length of life. Its early disintegration occurred when a missionary persuaded the inhabitants of the pa to make use of a sacred totara log that floated of its own volition in the neighbourhood of the Horomatangi Reef. The log was either a taniwha or a tipua and may well have been the notable taniwha Horomatangi. When it was hauled ashore and used in the construction of the church its tapu was still potent. The men who cut it up suffered misfortune and the church was soon disused and fell into decay.

Horomatangi also enters into a legend that links Ohinemutu by Lake Rotorua with Rotoaira, the lake that nestles between Tongariro and Pihanga. The taniwha Huru-kareao, who lived in the lake, was a relative of Horomatangi. He had taken the inhabitants of the lakeside pa under his protection and it is said that the men and women of this pa lived lives of such rectitude that Horomatangi was unable to find another hapu of equal reputation. The two taniwha entered into an arrangement to share responsibility for caring for these excellent people.

Having heard good reports of the pleasant springs at Ohinemutu, Hineutu, a young woman who belonged to the Rotoaira hapu, decided to visit the pa by the lakeside at Rotorua. She travelled north and stayed there for a short time. The Arawa people of Ohinemutu heaped indignities upon her, for they had little respect for the southern hapu. They had not heard of the favour with which her people were regarded by the taniwha of Taupo and Rotoaira.

Unable to endure the taunts of the young men and women of Ohinemutu, Hineutu hurried back to her home and called for vengeance. The tohunga chanted incantations to summon Huru-kareao to the pa. The taniwha in turn called his relative from Lake Taupo. When they heard Hineutu's tale their indignation rose to such a pitch that they threw themselves about in the lake, with disastrous results. The pa at Rotoaira was engulfed by the waves. At Tokaanu the surging waters changed the channel of the river and submerged another pa on its banks.

Through Taupo-moana and over the hills and through the valleys the two taniwha sped northwards on their mission of vengeance. They were weary by the time they reached Ohinemutu. They plunged into Lake Rotorua but only half of the village was submerged and many of the inhabitants escaped.

There are three springs, one at Rotoaira, one at Tokaanu, and another at Ohinemutu, all of which are named Huru-kareao. At Motutaiko, Horomatangi lives in an underground cave. For many years he amused himself by upsetting passing canoes and satisfied his hunger by devouring their crews. Now he lies deep in his cave and contents himself with snapping harmlessly at the propellers of launches, the modern taniwha which prowl the lake today.

DENIZENS OF THE SEA

The ocean as well as the land was the bride of Rangi. In one account of the creation Rangi married Wainui-atea, who gave birth to Moana-nui. (Moana means sea or ocean; wai means water.) The seas were personified in Hine-moana and Wainui. Not surprisingly Papa had little love for her rival. In characteristic style Elsdon Best once wrote: "The Ocean Maid is spoken of as constantly assailing the Earth Mother, ever she attacks her; all bays, gulfs, inlets we see are 'te ngaunga a Hinemoana', the result of the gnawing of Hine-moana into the great body of Tuanuku, our universal mother. This aggression was noted by the Whanau-a-Rangi (Offspring of Rangi), who appointed Rakahore, Hine-tu-a-kirikiri, and Hine-one (personified forms of rock, gravel, and sand) to protect the flanks of the Earth Mother from being swallowed by Hine-moana. When the serried battalions of the Ocean Maid roll in, rank behind rank, to assault the Earth Mother, gaunt Rakahore faces them fearlessly, and they break in fury around him. Still they rush on, in wavering array, to hurl themselves in vain against the rattling armour of the Gravel Maid, or upon the smooth but immovable form of the Sand Maid. They budge not, but ever stand between Papa the Parentless and the fury of Hine-moana."

The origin of the tides is ascribed to Parata, a taniwha that lived far out in the ocean, drawing water in and out of its mouth. By means of the incantations of Ngatoro-i-rangi the *Arawa* canoe was nearly drawn into Te Waha-a-Parata (The Mouth of Parata) but escaped at the last moment.

Apart from whales and sharks, some of which have been described as taniwha, and have, on occasion, been well- or ill-disposed to mankind, there was a weird creature called marakihau. The carvers of the Bay of Plenty represented it as a figure with human body and head, a fish's tail, and a long, tubular tongue termed a ngongo. The marakihau was of gigantic proportions, for the tongue was used to draw canoes into its capacious mouth.

Nearer to the land the ponaturi, a malevolent marine counterpart of the patupaiarehe, were feared by coast dwellers. The ponaturi were closely related to the patupaiarehe. They shared their aversion to the sunshine and strong daylight, but were creatures of the sea who came ashore only at night. One of the best known Maori legends is the account of how the cult hero Rata rescued his father's bones from the ponaturi. In the following tale Kaumariki lost his friends and barely escaped with his life from these repellent creatures of the sea.

The bone fish-hook named Te Rama possessed the property of attracting fish from a great distance. It was coveted by Kaumariki who dared to violate its tapu. With the help of two friends, Tawhai and Kupe, he stole the sacred fish-hook. Fearing the owner's revenge, they set sail in a canoe and did not stop until they reached a lonely island far across the sea. The water near the shore was teeming with fish.

"Look!" Kaumariki shouted. "Te Rama is already at work. The fish are leaping towards it."

They decided to wait until the following day. Kaumariki collected a heap of driftwood, but Tawhai and Kupe decided to keep out the cold of the night by heaping sun-warmed sand over their bodies.

"The sand will grow cold long before dawn," Kaumariki warned. "A hot fire is the only way to drive out the demons of cold."

He dragged the firewood into a circle, set it alight and lay down in the centre.

He was awakened by cries of terror. Looking across the dull embers of his fire he saw his friends imprisoned in their bed of sand fighting vainly against a horde of weird creatures. Their skins were a greenish-white that glowed with putrescent light. Their fingers terminated in long claws with which they were tearing the skin from the helpless men.

Kaumariki piled dry wood on the fire, driving back the bolder ones who were advancing towards him. As soon as the flames died down the creatures rushed to attack him, retreating only as the frantic man fed the flames.

At daybreak the sea creatures disappeared into the sea. Kaumariki stepped cautiously over the charred timbers and went to the trenches where the bodies had been lying. There was no trace of his friends. Skin, flesh, blood, bones and hair had all been devoured. Kaumariki dared not face another night alone on the haunted island. He dragged the canoe into the water and headed for home.

On arrival at the pa he gave Te Rama back to its owner and admitted his offence. In view of what he had suffered, his theft was pardoned.

"I must avenge the death of my friends," he said. "Who will come with me? I need at least a hundred warriors and one of our largest war canoes."

"How can you ever overcome the ponaturi?" he was asked. "The bravest fighter is no match for the endless multitudes of the sea devils."

"If you do as I tell you we shall overcome them," Kaumariki replied. "Let the women collect raupo leaves and manuka stakes. We shall use them to build a whare on the island. While they are doing this you must cut down many trees and fashion the trunks into the shape of men."

Kaumariki took four gourds. He packed them with fungus and filled them with shark oil, intending to use them as lamps. When they were finished he wrapped them in bark covers.

The next day the heavily laden crew set off on its journey of revenge. As soon as it reached the island, everyone helped to unload the canoe and build a large whare. When it was completed the wooden effigies, wrapped in cloaks, were placed on the floor.

The shadows deepened. Kaumariki posted a warrior in each corner of the building with a lighted lamp in his hands. The bark covers shielded the flame. In

the subdued light it seemed as though many men were sleeping on the floor of the whare.

The remaining warriors sheltered inside a circle of fire that had been lit nearby. The hours passed slowly but everyone remained silent and alert. Towards midnight a whisper passed through the ranks of warriors. A dark shadow had appeared out of the water.

As 'it advanced up the beach the greenish-white skin of the ponaturi reflected the flames of the watchfire. It was joined by three more figures. The four ponaturi scouts, keeping well away from the fire, approached the whare. They peered through the open doorway, saw the motionless forms lying on the sandy floor and whispered, "Kei te moe! Asleep." Their leader turned and repeated loudly, "Kei te moe!"

Hundreds of ponaturi rushed up the beach, struggled through the doorway and fell on the cloaked forms. When they were all inside Kaumariki gave a shout. The four warriors who had been standing motionless in the corners of the whare pulled the shades from their lamps. The ponaturi were blinded by the light. Holding their hands over their eyes, they rushed blindly to and fro, searching for the door. In the confusion the four warriors slipped outside.

Kaumariki barred the door and signalled to the warriors to apply torches to the brushwood walls. A few terrified sea creatures managed to escape through the blazing walls. The rest were burned to death in a blaze of light and burning heat as the flames soared upwards, transforming the whare into a fiery revenge for the death of Tawhai and Kupe.

Reference has been made several times to transformations and the difficulty of placing supernatural beings into specific categories. Such is true of Pania and Moremore.

Pania was a young woman of the sea — not a ponaturi, but with the mind and appearance of a mortal woman. There is no term by which she can be identified.

The land had already exercised a strange fascination for Pania. Every evening she left her home in the sea and lay concealed among the flax bushes at the foot of the Hukarere cliff where Napier stands today, returning to her own people at dawn.

In the half-light of dusk Karitoki, a young chief from a neighbouring village, noticed her as he came to drink the water of a spring. He went over to her, took her by the hand and led her gently to his home. The door closed behind them. Pania was content to remain with this man of the land until the stars grew dim before the dawn light. She left the arms of her sleeping husband, pressed her face gently against his tattooed cheek, and swam through the breakers back to her own people.

Each day as the light waned he waited her coming. Together they made their way past the flax bushes and the spring to their home. As the sea breeze dried her glistening body Karitoki felt the warmth of love welling up and reaching towards him in his strange sea bride.

A year went by. Pania gave birth to a boy, a tiny bundle of humanity she named Moremore (Hairless). Each morning she left him with her husband. As the chief cared for his son during the day he began to fear that the child might inherit the characteristics of his sea ancestors. He went to the tohunga to ask how he could keep his wife and child with him permanently.

"It should not be difficult," the tohunga assured him, "Wait until they are both asleep. You must then place cooked food on their bodies. They will never return to the sea again."

It was perhaps understandable that the tohunga had assumed that Pania was a ponaturi, or at least had some affinity with these supernatural creatures. The assumption was not correct. In trying to keep his loved ones with him Karitoki lost both son and wife. When she was touched by the tapu-dispelling food Pania took her son in her arms and walked into the sea. She had no wish to leave her husband, but men and women of land and sea have different natures and different customs.

Pania became a rock, which was often frequented by fishermen. In her left armpit the tamure (snapper) swam, and between her thighs the hapuku (groper). Moremore, the hairless one, was transformed into a taniwha. In form he resembled a shark that made its home by the reef off the Hukarere shore and in the inner harbour by the mouth of the Ahuriri River.

In spite of the vast gulf that lies between men and women of alien culture Pania longed as desperately for her lover as Karitoki yearned for her. It is a sad story of lovers parted by conditions over which they had no control. At ebb tide Pania could be seen below the reef with her arms stretched out vainly towards her lover.

FABULOUS BIRDS

Aotearoa was the home of that great bird the moa, which, within the memory of the Maori people, roamed the plains and was hunted for food until it was exterminated; but for some unknown reason the fabulous birds of the land were always provided with wings.

The poua-kai may well have been the extinct eagle of the South Island. It lived on the summit of Tawera (Mount Torlesse) and preyed on the people of the plains. From its eyrie the man-eating bird maintained a constant lookout. As soon as it saw a party of travellers it spread its wings, swooped down, and carried them away to its nest, where it devoured them at leisure.

Ruru, a noted bird-hunter, was chosen to lead an expedition against the man-eating bird. There are several versions of the strategies he employed to snare it. In one of the more plainly embroidered accounts he chose fifty men to assist him. At Ruru's direction they cut a large quantity of manuka poles and carried them to a pool at the foot of the mountain. The poles were laced together to form a net over the water. The warriors crouched beneath it. Ruru lured the poua-kai to the wooden net and its legs were entangled in the poles. The men who were hidden underneath dragged them down and killed the helpless bird with their weapons.

In an even simpler form of the legend the poua-kai attacked a red-haired man, but its claws became entangled in his rough flax cape. The bird was unable to defend itself and was beaten to death by a band of warriors who had been lying in wait.

Some significance was attached to the fact that the object of the bird's attack was a red-head, and a saying was later applied to anyone with red hair: "Ha! The decoy of poua-kai!"

One of the best-known bird legends was that of a flying moa which conveyed Pou-rangahua, a man of great mana, from Hawaiki to Aotearoa. The chief had gone to the homeland to obtain kumara for his young son. On his return he was conveyed on the back of the bird and so established this important crop in New Zealand (see page 37).

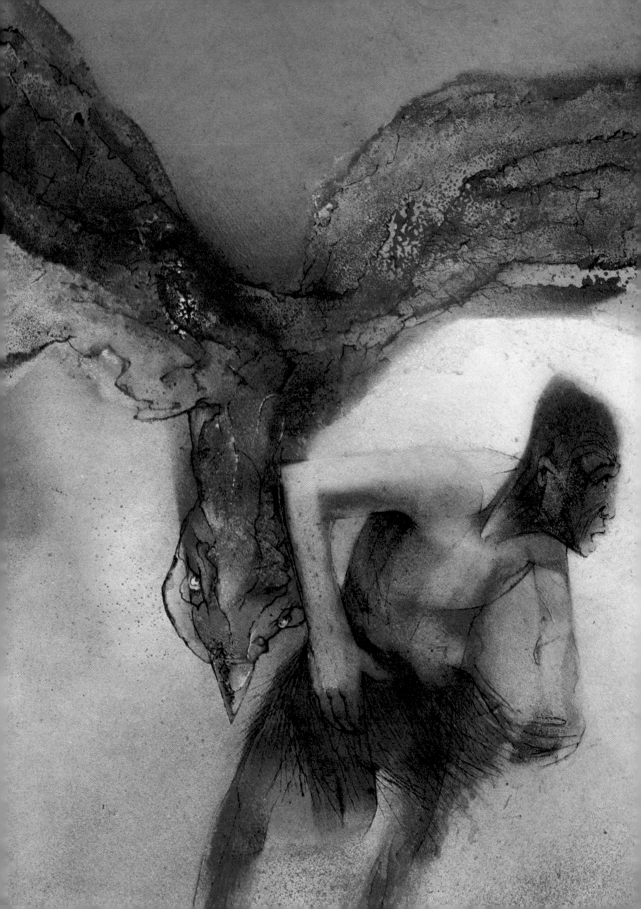

When Kupe, the Polynesian explorer, came to Aotearoa more than a thousand years ago, he brought with him two birds. Rupe, the wood-pigeon, was given the task of finding forest seeds and fruit. Te Kawau-a-toru was told to seek out all the tidal rivers and inlets. On arrival at the heads of the Manukau harbour, Te Kawau was sent out and came back with the report that the currents were not unduly strong.

Having proved its value, Kupe sent the bird to swim in all the rivers and harbours on the west coast of the North Island. In so doing the bird developed great strength in its wings and legs, and longed to find a current that would extend its powers to the full. Even the tidal rips of Raukawa, which men later called Cook Strait, were unable to daunt the shag.

While Kupe was sheltering in Worser Bay in Port Nicholson, Te Kawau met several birds that had come from the South Island.

"Do you know of any places where the currents of ocean or rivers of the land are strong?" Te Kawau asked. "I have conquered all the waters of this island."

"There are currents you'll never be able to overcome in our island," they replied proudly. "You must come and see for yourself."

Te Kawau sought its master's permission, and promised to return and tell him what it had found. Kupe consented and settled for a while at Rimurapa, which the Pakeha know as Sinclair Head, with his daughters.

When Te Kawau-a-toru, accompanied by the birds of the South Island, reached the narrow channel between Rangitoto (D'Urville Island) and the mainland, its attention was drawn to the water which swept through in an angry, swirling torrent.

"Ah! This is nothing to what you will see in a little while," the birds told Te Kawau. "Wait till the tide is full."

"That's the reason I came," said Te Kawau. "If I am able to overcome the tide rips it will prove that they are weak and have no strength against my master's canoe."

They flew down and inspected the water closely.

"The current is flowing faster," they cried. "The time has come for you to try it. Your strength will never prevail against the torrents of Rangitoto."

Te Kawau swept down and touched the tidal rip with the tip of a wing, testing it as a bather might feel the water with his toes. The current was stronger than the bird thought. It caught his wing and held it so firmly that it was forced to its knees. Te Kawau advanced the other wing, but the birds cried out in shrill alarm, "You will be killed!"

Te Kawau was not frightened, even though one of its wings was stretched from one side of the channel to the other, held in the fierce grip of the water. It tried to raise itself by flapping the free wing, but in vain. Inexorably the flapping wing was forced down to the racing torrent. It surged round the gallant bird, swept it off its feet, and whirled it round like a chip of wood in the eddy of a stream. Te Kawau kept on struggling, but the wing was broken. The brave one of Kupe had at last met its match.

If Te Kawau-a-toru had won the struggle, the channel would have been tamed, and women could have paddled their canoes through in safety.

But the great-hearted bird was drowned. Fierce tides race through the perilous passage. It is known to the Pakeha as French Pass in honour of another brave one who met the challenge in a white-winged vessel.

The black-winged Kawau remains there for all time, petrified by an act of defiance into a boulder that still challenges the racing tides and rips of the pass that was named to commemorate the French navigator who broke its power long after Kupe left these enchanted islands.

THE COMING
OF POUNAMU

As gold to the Pakeha, so was greenstone, or pounamu, to the Maori. It was intensely hard. It could be ground to a fine edge and was more durable than any other stone. Its translucent colour added beauty to ornaments such as hei-tiki and ear pendants. In this respect it not infrequently served two purposes. A disused adze blade could be fashioned as a tiki. It seems probable that the squat shape with inturned legs and slanted head originated from the shape of an adze head. Possession of tools made of this durable jade was largely responsible for the considerable advance in the art of carving in Aotearoa compared with other Polynesian islands. Greenstone was also an important item of barter between South and North Island tribes. Round its origin and discovery clustered many fabulous legends.

Captain Cook mentioned in his journal: "... we were told a hundred fabulous stories about this stone, not one of which carried with it the least probability of truth, though some of their most sensible men would have us believe them. One of these stories is, that this stone is originally a fish, which they strike with a gig in the water, tie a rope to it, and drag it to the shore, to which they fasten it, and it afterwards becomes a stone. As they all agree that it is fished out of a large lake, or collection of waters, the most probable conjecture is, that it is brought from the mountains, and deposited in the water by the torrents. This lake is called by the native *Tavai Poenammoo*; that is, the Water of Green Talc; and it is only the adjoining part of the country, and not the whole southern island of New Zealand, that is known by the name which hath been given to it on my chart."

One of the legends that Cook may have heard is of men who went to the West Coast fiords in search of greenstone. They discovered a large piece in the sea. One canoe took up a position behind it, and one on each side. They drove it southwards along the coast, endeavouring to force it ashore. The fish-like pounamu constantly eluded them. It was not until they reached Bluff that they managed to secure it. The supposed fish-like greenstone is now Motupiu (Dog Island). Local belief was that the island was supported on three greenstone pillars.

To go further back into the mythological past, Poutini was the ancestor of pounamu. Whatu-o-Poutini (Stone of Poutini) and Whatu-o-Tangaroa are poetical terms for greenstone. As the Stone of Tangaroa, god of the sea, its connections with fish become apparent. In one of the several genealogies of Tangaroa, the sea god married Te Anu-matao (The Chilly Cold), who gave birth to four personifications: Pounamu, Poutini, Te Whatukura-a-Tangaroa, and Te Whatu-i-kura, each of whom was a fish.

Poutini was the guardian of Pounamu. In the distant Moana-kura a quarrel arose between Poutini and Tutunui, personification of the whale family. Tutunui wished that the ocean be reserved for his own kindred, fish and shellfish. Poutini demanded that Pounamu be allowed to remain there. It was an irreconcilable difference, for Poutini contended that Pounamu was a fish, while Tutunui maintained that he was merely a stone.

Tutunui enlisted the aid of Hine-tu-a-hoanga, the personification of sandstone and a traditional enemy of Pounamu. (Sandstone is the abrasive used in the manufacture of greenstone implements, weapons, and ornaments.) Pursued by Hine-tu-a-hoanga, Poutini brought Pounamu to the shores of Aotearoa. A landing was made on Tuhua (Mayor Island). Poutini would have been content to remain there permanently, but Tuhua was the home of two further enemies, Mata (flint or quartz) and Tuhua (obsidian).

Poutini and Pounamu, who may be described collectively as the Greenstone People, fled to East Cape. Here they were opposed by Whaiapu (another form of flint) and Tua-a-hoanga, who appears to be closely related to Hine of that name.

Relentlessly the Greenstone People were pursued and driven from one resting place to another until at last they reached the west coast of the South Island, where they made a determined stand against the Sandstone People.

Pungapunga, the wife of Poutini, was killed. Her name was perpetuated in a light-coloured variety of greenstone. At this point the collective term Greenstone People has become appropriate, for in the battle at Arahura many of their chiefs were captured and taken away as slaves of the Sandstone People. Others took refuge beneath a waterfall, and here, in the river at Arahura, Pounamu took its permanent form as a mother-lode of greenstone.

The waterfall was guarded by a moa which was later killed by the early explorer Ngahue, the companion of Kupe on his epoch-making voyage to New Zealand. As Ngahue is credited with taking moa flesh and greenstone back to Hawaiki, it may be well to include an alternative version of the pounamu legend.

In this tale, Poutini was a block of greenstone that belonged to Ngahue. Whaiapu was a flint owned by Hine-tu-a-hoanga. Hine found it difficult to reduce the unyielding greenstone and drove Ngahue away from Hawaiki. Ngahue arrived at Tuhua with his precious greenstone but, frightened by the appearance of the people who lived there, he made a hasty departure. Traversing the east coast, he became aware of Kanioro "grinding away on the land". Kanioro is a term used to describe the cutting of greenstone by grinding a groove with sand and water. Eventually Ngahue managed to evade his pursuer and took refuge at

Arahura, where he broke off a piece to take back to Hawaiki. The famous adzes Tutauru and Hauhau-te-rangi were fashioned from it and, centuries later, were used to fell the trees from which the *Arawa* and other canoes were made.

To complete a trilogy of somewhat confusing and contradictory legends, we introduce Tama-ahua who came from Whangaparaoa and Whangamata in pursuit of his wives, one of whom was Waitaika and who had been abducted by Poutini. Poutini, the pounamu canoe, was afraid of Mata-a-tuhua, the obsidian of Mayor Island, and for this reason had fled southwards.

Tama-ahua used a popular device to discover where his wives had gone. He kept throwing his teka (dart) in front of him and followed it to the place where it fell. The first throw took him to Taupo-moana. The dart kept silent, thus informing Tama-ahua that his wife was not there. The second flight ended at Taranaki, where it crashed against a rock. Tama-ahua then knew that the teka had discovered the path his wife had taken. A further throw and the teka landed at Farewell Spit. Successive casts brought it to Arahura, where Tama-ahua found the sail of Poutini, which had been wrecked on the inhospitable coast, and knew that his quest was coming to an end.

Tama-ahua made offerings to the atua in the hope that they would restore his wives to life, but his slave had the misfortune to burn his fingers on the cooked food. On licking his fingers to relieve the pain, the tapu was destroyed and the gifts rendered ineffective.

Finally, the legend of Tamatea is told to explain why different kinds of greenstone are found in the South Island. Tamatea-pokai-whenua (or possibly Tama-ki-te-rangi or Tama-ahua) had been deserted by his three wives. He sailed down the east coast of the South Island in the *Tairea* canoe, rounded the south coast, and went northward until he came to Piopiotahi (Milford Sound). As he searched the shores of the south his clothes were torn to shreds which grew into kiekie and other plants, thus giving rise to a term for vegetation, Te Pokeka-a-Tama (The Rough Cloak of Tama).

At Anita Bay he found one of his wives, who had been turned into greenstone. As he bent over her hot tears streamed down his face, dropping into the translucent stone where they can be seen in the type of greenstone known as tangiwai (weeping water). Tangiwai and her children had all been turned into greenstone, but the younger ones had scrambled over the hills and made their home further inland.

Tama left his petrified wife on the beach and went further north until he came to the Arahura River. He travelled up-river until he came to a place where there were many stones and a constant murmur of voices. He did not recognise his other two wives in these enchanted stones, not knowing that their canoe had capsized and that the ledge of greenstone in the river was in reality both the canoe and his petrified wives.

Tama abandoned his canoe and, accompanied by his slave Tumuaki, he stopped to cook some birds. It was here that the slave burned his fingers and violated tapu, thus preventing any further possibility of bringing the women back to life. Some of the most precious greenstone contains flaws known as tutae koka (excrement of the birds that Tumuaki cooked).

TOHUNGA

The tohunga occupied an important place in the economy of everyday life as well as in the more esoteric elements of Maori thought. Basically he was an expert, whether in the construction of canoes, house building, carving or other occupations.

As the natural and supernatural were so intermingled and interdependent the tohunga was a necessary connecting channel or medium between men and the atua. In order to exercise his functions as a guide to lesser men a word-perfect knowledge of the karakia that ensured the co-operation of the gods was essential. A war party would not dare to set forth on a punitive expedition without a tohunga to interpret the omens that pointed to success.

In this section however we are concerned with the priestly function of the tohunga. The period spent in the whare wananga was long and arduous, no matter what grade of teaching was involved. There were several classes of tohunga, and amongst them were specialists such as tohunga-tatai-arorangi who interpreted the passage and appearance of the stars, tohunga makutu or whaiwhaia who used the power of black magic to kill, and tohunga matakite who foretold the future.

Within the whare wananga, the school of occult knowledge, the highest class was the whare kura, the school which has already been noted as the home of the baskets of knowledge brought to mankind by Tane. Historical traditions, legends, karakia and the rituals pertaining to war and agriculture were amongst the subjects taught in the whare kura and at the completion of the course, which might occupy several years, tohunga were required to demonstrate their powers.

Although many Pakeha think of the tohunga as "witch doctors", and know something of the way they exercised their power, we must not overlook their influence in government. The priestly function was beneficent. Every action of the tohunga was governed by tapu, the sacredness and strict order of procedure that ensured that men did not unwittingly offend the gods.

The ultimate test of a graduate of the whare maire, or school of "black magic", was his ability to kill a man by the power of mind alone. Lesser men might destroy a dog or a bird but the tohunga whaiwhaia who had gained complete mastery of the powers of makutu was able to project his power over men and women.

A macabre story from the mysterious Urewera country illustrates the depths to which tohunga who dabbled in black magic descended. Kohuru had passed all tests except the final one and he had fallen in love with Titia-i-te-rangi, the daughter of Tawhaki, a tohunga of Urewera. Tawhaki was an adept in the arts of makutu, greatly feared by his people, intolerant and vengeful, and known far and wide as a tohunga whaiwhaia. When Kohuru asked Tawhaki for his daughter in marriage, the old tohunga refused on the grounds that he was immature and unworthy of his daughter.

Kohuru then consulted Tatua-nui, another tohunga of great mana.

"The young hawk may fly further than its parent," Tatua-nui said enigmatically. "Remain with me for three months and we shall see how far you have progressed."

Unaware of the dark heart of the old tohunga and that he had recognised the young man's latent powers and planned to make use of them, Kohuru agreed.

At the end of three months Tatua said, "There is nothing more to teach you. The time has come to put you to the proof. The test will be made at Manukau. I shall go with you to observe the result."

Unfortunately the training he had received had altered Kohuru's nature. Tatua had insisted that tapu must be observed strictly on the journey but Kohuru was not willing to deny himself food and, contrary to Tatua's instructions, he hid a stick freshly cut from a tree and a bundle of fernroot untouched by human hands under his cloak.

Tatua-nui, old and corpulent, found the journey without food or drink a trying experience. Kohuru secretly planted his stick in the ground at each camping place and suspended the fernroot from it so that he could eat without his hands touching it. Although in this way he did not violate tapu he said nothing of his subterfuge to his mentor.

On the third day the old tohunga died of hunger and thirst. With his last breath he urged Kohuru to destroy the chief Matuku who was an old enemy and rival. This in fact had been his purpose in training Kohuru in the deadly arts of makutu.

The young man hastened to Matuku's pa and concealed himself in the fern beneath the palisades. In the cold light of dawn he saw Matuku emerge from his whare and climb the watch tower to see whether any strangers had entered his territory. Kohuru concentrated the powers of darkness in his mind and hurled them at the unsuspecting tohunga. A gleam of triumph flared in his eyes as Matuku jerked and fell backwards.

Kohuru had graduated in the black art with full honours and no longer feared the father of Titia. But on his return to the Urewera Tawhaki was still obdurate.

"Would you accept a tohunga as powerful as Matuku for your son-in-law?" Kohuru asked.

"Yes, there is a man indeed," Tawhaki said.

"Alas," said Kohuru, "he is dead."

"How did he die?" Tawhaki asked in surprise.

"It was I who killed him," Kohuru said proudly. "Just take a look at these. They are proof that I am more powerful than Matuku and more fitted to wed your daughter."

He placed a taiaha, a hei-tiki and a shark's tooth ear pendant that he had taken from Matuku's body in front of Tawhaki.

The older tohunga turned them over and examined them closely. "Yes," he said at last, "these are Matuku's, but what proof have I that it was you who was responsible for his death?"

"These are the proof," Kohuru said impatiently.

"Ah, but I must observe your power for myself before I grant your request. Look, Kohuru. The women are beginning to leave the kumara plantation. They are approaching the pa. Cast your spell on the first one to set foot on the path. If she is dead by the time we reach her I shall give my daughter to you."

They waited until one of the women stepped on to the path. Kohuru concentrated all his powers as he muttered the chant of death and they saw a young woman fall to the ground as Matuku had fallen a few weeks earlier.

Kohuru raced down the path and picked up the body to show Tawhaki that she was dead.

He had indeed triumphed in the dreadful magic of the black art, but he had lost his intended bride as well, for the woman he had killed was Titia-i-te-rangi.

Not infrequently the powers of rival tohunga were put to the test, and a conflict developed to prove which was the one most thoroughly versed in the arts of the whare maire. Such is the story of Hakawau and Paawa.

Both the tohunga had fallen in love with Rona, a woman of charm and beauty. Hakawau lived far away at Kawhia and had never declared his love – nor had Paawa, an evil tohunga who had power over many atua. Seizing an opportunity

80

when the girl was not closely guarded, the tohunga snatched her away from her home and imprisoned her in his own pa.

As soon as he learnt of Rona's abduction her brother Korokia hastily assembled a war party and set out to rescue her. The men were afraid of Paawa's unearthly powers and crept through the bush, avoiding the forest trails. They hoped to take the tohunga's pa by surprise. On reaching the edge of the forest they closed their ranks and ran across the open space in front of the pa, but before they could reach it some madness seized them. Many fell lifeless to the ground, others turned on their friends and fierce fighting broke out among them. Of the large party of men who set out on the war path only one escaped. Korokia was the sole survivor of the gallant band.

He returned sadly to his home and sent a message to Hakawau, who was noted for his prowess in battle, to lead another taua against Paawa. The young chief was anxious to help his friend and to rescue the girl for whom he had a secret affection, but he knew that he was no match for Paawa.

"You must be patient," he said to Korokia. "I will go to the warlocks of the Urewera and learn the secrets of their black art. Then and only then can we hope to subdue Paawa."

It was many months before he returned from his arduous course of makutu. He went directly to Korokia's pa and said, "I have learnt the karakia that will overcome Paawa's evil, the magic that will grind his face in the dust."

It was a small force that followed Hakawau and Korokia, for few able-bodied men were left in the village. They made no attempt to hide themselves from the enemy and soon arrived in sight of Paawa's fortress. Hakawau went forward slowly. His warriors saw Paawa standing alone on the watch tower, but Hakawau's trained eyes could also see a host of evil atua trooping out of the gate and converging on his men. Summoning all his strength and drawing on the knowledge he had learnt from the experts of Tuhoe in the gloomy Urewera forests, he chanted the karakia that would summon their atua to his aid.

On the field of battle there were only two men who could see the ghostly warriors closing in to the attack. The cries of contending spirits, the thud of weapons, the hoarse panting of the fighters, and the moans of the wounded rang in the ears of Hakawau and Paawa. For a time the issue was in doubt but at last the atua of Urewera routed the spirits that Paawa had summoned to his aid.

Hakawau returned to his men. "Let us go forward," he said "The time of vengeance has come."

One of the boldest warriors, whom none could accuse of cowardice, caught his arm. "O Hakawau!" he said, "I know that you are fearless but I tremble at your command. I can fight with flesh and blood, but the ghostly wairua will kill us before we can reach the outer palisades of the pa."

Hakawau looked at him in surprise.

"The fighting is over," he said. "I have been watching it. The atua of Paawa are dead. See for yourself."

He led the way, his men following reluctantly. They had seen nothing of the conflict, but they trusted their leader. He led them through the unmanned

mazes of the palisades. Paawa was no longer standing on the watch tower. He
had seen the defeat of his atua. His mana had been taken from him. He stood
with bowed head.

Hakawau strode up to him. "Your power has gone, Paawa," he said sternly.
"Your karakia availed little against mine. I will not kill you. I have shamed
you this day. Remember in humility that your life was spared by Hakawau. You
are no longer a tohunga, nor a rangatira. You are now a tutua, a person of
mean birth.

"And now, where is Rona?" he demanded abruptly.

The discredited tohunga meekly led his opponent to a whare and slid back
the door. Rona came out. She was indeed a beauty, whom all men might desire.
Her skin was fair, her limbs were rounded, she was graceful in all her movements
– and in her eyes was a soft light of love for the young tohunga of Kawhia.

GIANTS

Legends of men of great stature vary from enormous beings like Matau to men like Tuhourangi who was six feet to his armpits and nine feet to the top of his head. When he shouted to his slaves from the shore of Rotorua he could be heard six kilometres away on the island of Mokoia. Tuhourangi was out-matched by Te Pute of Ngapuhi, whose eyes were as big as saucers, and whose sneeze could be heard from Punakitere to Kaikohe, a distance of nearly ten kilometres.

Toangina was another of giant stature. He was the scourge of the lower reaches of the Waikato River. When a canoe came in sight he swung himself from the bank on a long vine, plucked a victim from the canoe and killed him with a single blow from his fist. In this way he had slain the well-known chief Korongoi, cut up his body, and displayed the dismembered limbs as a warning to others.

Korongoi's son Te Horeta, though normally a brave warrior, was too faint-hearted to face up to Toangina until, at the incessant urging of his wife, he assembled a party of fighting men. They attacked the giant in his home until he was forced to flee. Te Horeta was in the vanguard of the pursuers. The giant turned at bay and in the conflict, the young chief's taiaha was broken. The jagged end pierced the puku of Toangina and so ended his reign of terror.

The original name of Lake Wakatipu in Central Otago was Whakatipua – the hollow of the demon. "Whaka" is a South Island variant of "Whanga", a harbour or hollow.

The tipua was a giant named Matau, who stole the beautiful girl Manata from

her father's home on the plains. Her lover, Matakauri, set out in search of her and found her seated by the bank of a river.

"I have come to take you home," he said as he clasped her in his arms.

"Alas, my lover, I can never escape. Matau has tied me to him with a cord made from the skin of his two-headed dogs. It can never be broken."

Matakauri smiled confidently. He began to saw the cord with his maripi but the knife made no impression on the tough hide. Manata bent over it and, as her tears dropped onto the leather thong, it dissolved and she was free. Holding hands, the lovers floated downstream until they reached the girl's home.

Knowing that his bride would never be safe from the giant, Matakauri determined to kill him. He waited until the northwest wind blew across the mountains and then set out on his quest. He soon found the place where Matau was sleeping soundly on a bed of bracken in the vast bowl of the hills. Creeping quietly round the giant he set fire to the dry fern. Fanned by the wind, the flames licked Matau's sides causing him to draw up his legs. Before he could regain consciousness he was suffocated by the dense smoke.

The flames were fed by the running fat. His body sank deep into the earth until it formed a vast chasm many kilometres in length and several hundred metres in depth. The whole body was consumed and reduced to ashes – all except the heart, which continued to beat strongly in its narrow tomb.

The wind died. The rain fell in torrents, pouring into the newly made gulf from many streams. The heat of the fire had melted the snow on the mountains, which fed the swiftly flowing rivers that poured into the Whaka of Matau. It was filled to the brim and remained a lake that has retained for all time the shape of the giant who drew up his knees when he felt the fierce heat of the burning bracken.

His heart still beats far below the surface of the water – sometimes fiercely, so that the lake is tormented by waves that beat angrily against the shore. More often the surface is placid as the water slowly rises and ebbs to the gentle heart beat of Matau the tipua. That is the story of the mysterious rise and fall of Lake Wakatipu – a phenomenon for which the Pakeha has no convincing explanation.

OGRESSES

In addition to patupaiarehe, taniwha and ponaturi the legendary world of the Maori was peopled with a number of different kinds of supernatural creatures – tipua or goblins, maero or wild men of the forests, giants, ogres and ogresses. Tales of Maori ogresses or witches were told at night, to the huge enjoyment of the listener – though small children may well have clung to their mothers while the fitful flames caused dark shadows to pounce on the cowering tamariki.

Amongst the most horrifying yet popular tales was that of Ruruhi-kerepo, the old blind woman whose body bristled with bones like a porcupine fish.

Five women left their kainga to walk through the forest. Being young and full of high spirits, they made fun of Ruruhi-kerepo when they met her.

"Look!" one of the girls said. "Here is a ruruhi (old woman)."

"You must never say that to me," Ruruhi-kerepo said, as the girls danced around her. "I am not really old. Call me matua keke (aunt)."

As the girls quietened down Ruruhi challenged them to see who could climb the highest in a nearby tree. When they were all clinging to the branches she cackled, "Sit there, my nieces. You are lovely girls – so lovely that I could eat you. Each of you would make a tasty mouthful."

She began to shake the branches. The girls saw with dismay that the old woman's hands were strong and hairy with claw-like nails. The nearest girl was shaken off her perch. With a scream she fell into Ruruhi's arms. Opening a mouth that looked like the jaw of a taniwha the old blind woman bit off the girl's head, dropped it on the ground, and swallowed her body whole. One by one the girls were caught, decapitated, and swallowed.

That night there was much speculation as to what had happened to the girls. At first light a party of young men set out in search of them. Suddenly their leader stopped with a look of horror on his face. On the path at his feet lay the heads of the missing girls.

Anger burned fiercely in the breasts of the young men. They spread out and searched diligently through the bush. One of them saw Ruruhi-kerepo. When he came close to her she looked harmless enough so he asked her if she had seen the missing girls. Her gnarled hands shot out and drew him to her. She bit off his head and swallowed his body as she had done to the girls.

His companions saw what had happened. They surrounded Ruruhi. Seeing there was no hope of escape she dropped her cloak to the ground. To their horror and disgust the warriors realised that their clubs would be useless, for the bones of the men and women she had swallowed projected from her body like spines. But death was near. The men drew back and thrust their spears through Ruruhi-kerepo until she bristled with spears as well as bones.

Te Ruahine-mata-maori was unlike other ogresses who were notable for their repulsive appearance, for she was "the old woman with an ordinary face."

The chief Paowa was a famous traveller and explorer. On one of his voyages he landed on a distant shore and was greeted by Te Ruahine, who invited him

to partake of a meal. She took a basket of kumara from her stone pit and placed them in the earth oven. While they were cooking Paowa asked for a drink of water. In spite of her attractive appearance the chief recognised that she was an ogress and determined to outwit her. When she left her whare he bewitched the spring, causing it to dry up. She went to a pool of water but found only dry, cracked mud. Wherever she went the usual sources of water appeared to be exhausted.

Te Ruahine realised the Paowa had seen through her pretence of hospitality and understood that she intended to harm him. Looking back at her house she saw a column of smoke rising in the air. There was no sign of Paowa or of the canoe in which he had come.

She sat down and sang mournfully:

Let my house be burned,
But let my store remain.
Let my house of enchantment be burned,
But let my fences remain.
Let my filth-pot be burned.
But let my dogs remain.

The ogress called her dogs and asked them where her visitor had gone. They followed the man-scent down to the waters, sniffed among the seaweed, and pointed their noses towards the horizon. Te Ruahine was satisfied. She placed some kura under her armpits, threw off her cloak, and waded into the sea. The power of the sacred red ochre enabled her to swim under water with incredible speed. After travelling in this manner for several kilometres, she came up to the surface and looked around. There was the canoe and, close at hand, the shore of a strange land. She submerged quietly and came up close to the canoe. Paowa had been keeping a careful watch while his men were paddling the canoe. When he saw her head and shoulders rising above the waves he urged the crew to paddle quickly to the shore.

The canoe bounded forward, but Te Ruahine-mata-maori drove onward with the speed of a waka taua, the water surging against her breasts, her legs threshing like the flukes of a sperm whale. She stretched out her hand to grasp the topstrake of the canoe. Paowa shouted a last command to his men to turn the canoe and paddle for their lives. As it left he jumped overboard and swam swiftly to the shore.

Paowa ran up the beach and took refuge in a cave, frantically piling boulders across the entrance while the ogress crossed the sand. By the time she reached the cave the barricade was firmly in position. She scratched at it vainly and then sat down in front of it.

Inside the cave Paowa busied himself kindling a flame with his fire drill. When the flames took hold of the dried grass and seaweed he added sticks of driftwood and roasted food on the hot stones. When it was ready he called to Te Ruahine, "Old woman, where are you?"

"I am here, Paowa, waiting for you. You can't escape."

"I don't want to escape," he replied. "See, I've cooked some food for you. Now you can share a meal with me."

He pushed a few morsels between the stones. She snatched them and stuffed them into her mouth.

"Well, my mokopuna, that was a nice morsel, but I expect a proper meal from you."

"Don't be impatient," Paowa said, "There's plenty left. Shut your eyes and open your mouth wide."

When her eyes were closed, Paowa broke down the barrier at the mouth of the cave and threw a red hot boulder into her cavernous mouth. Te Ruahine swallowed it and fell to the ground. Paowa came warily out of the cave and bent over her. The dreaded ogress was dead. He touched her and lightning flashed from her armpits.

"Aha! The kura!" Paowa exclaimed.

He scooped it out and crawled into a hollow log lying close by. Then, by the power of the sacred kura, the log slid down the beach and propelled itself to his distant home, where his men received him as one returned from the dead.

The ogre of Mount Tarawera, although of ancient ancestry, is believed to have been alive and active less than a hundred years ago.

Tama-o-hoi was a chief of the tangata whenua, the first people to come to Aotearoa. When later arrivals settled in the thermal regions he frequently left his lair on Mount Tarawera to waylay, kill, and eat unwary travellers. As the victims belonged mainly to the Rotorua and Taupo tribes, Ngatoro-i-rangi, the priest of the *Arawa* canoe in which they had arrived, came to their aid. He climbed the mountain and stamped on the summit, which burst open and formed a huge chasm. Then the wise old tohunga thrust Tama into it, closed the opening, and so imprisoned the ogre.

For centuries Tama lay asleep, deep within the mountain, biding his time — until that fateful night in 1886 when the peaks Wahanga and Ruawahia erupted, claiming the lives of many Maori and Pakeha, and scattering boiling mud and ash over the green countryside. The mysterious being who caused the eruption, said many people, was Tama-o-hoi.

The ancient gods have not yet vanished from the land of the Maori for beliefs that are as germane to the land as the vegetation that covers it cannot be completely banished from the mind. After the Tarawera eruption Sophia, one of the most celebrated Maori guides, placed on record that "on Tarawera mountain there was a quantity of honey made by wild bees. No one ought to have touched it, as everything was tapued; but some young Maori men went up the mountain and took the honey, filling up billies and other vessels with it, and they brought it all away to Te Ariki, and some to Rotomahana, where they gave it to the old chief Rangihehuwa, who lived at the foot of the Pink Terraces. Now I was going to guide my visitors round the Terraces, and when we landed from the boats I saw old chief Rangihehuwa, and he offered me some of the honey; but I said, 'No, thank you,' for I knew it was tapued; therefore it would be wrong to take it. For had not the two old wise men of the tribe shown me over the mountain when I first came to Tarawera from the Bay of Islands, and did we not see Tama-o-hoi's cave, and in it his big comb with which he used to comb his hair? It was lying on a stone in the cave. And did not the old men with white hair tell me everything on Tarawera was tapu? So I had not forgotten their warning, and when Rangihehuwa wanted me to take his honey I said, 'No.' I would not have it or let my people take it either, for I knew the danger, so would have nothing to do with it.

"It is strange but true, every one of those people that ate of the tapued honey, every soul, perished in the eruption of Tarawera that took place very soon after; but I and my people, who did not touch it, were all saved; and so we came safely and thankfully out of the great disaster of 1886."

GLOSSARY

While most Maori words and phrases are explained as they appear in the text, the following are either sufficiently well known or occur too frequently for repeated definition.

Aotearoa New Zealand
Ariki Chief
Atua God
Hangi Earth oven in which food is cooked by hot stones
Hapu Sub-tribe
Hawaiki Original home of the Maori people
Hei-tiki Carved neck-pendant
Iwi Tribe
Kainga Unfortified village, settlement
Kaumatua Elder
Kehua Ghost
Koauau Flute
Kokiri Spear
Kokowai Red ochre
Kumara Kind of sweet potato
Kura Red ochre
Maero Monstrous wild man of the bush
Makutu Bewitch; witchcraft, spell
Mana Prestige, influence
Maripi Knife
Mere Short flat weapon of stone or greenstone
Moa Extinct giant flightless bird
Mokopuna grandchild
Pa Fortified village
Pakeha New Zealander of European (usually British) descent

Patupaiarehe Legendary inhabitant of the bush; "fairy"
Ponaturi Fabulous sea-dwelling being
Pounamu Greenstone
Puku Stomach, abdomen
Putorino Flute
Rangatira Chief; noble
Taiaha Long wooden weapon with pointed "tongue" at one end
Tamariki Children
Taniwha Fabulous monster, usually aquatic
Tapu Sacred; forbidden; restricted; sacredness, restriction; to impose such a restriction
Taua War party
Tipua Strange or supernatural object or being, such as a goblin; enchanted
Tohunga Expert; priest; wizard
Tuna Eel
Tutua A person of low degree
Umu Earth oven
Wairua Spirit, soul
Waka Canoe
Waka taua War canoe
Wananga Learning, knowledge, especially of the occult arts
Wharau Hut, rough shelter
Whare House

OTHER REED BOOKS

TALES OF THE MAORI
James Cowan
From the turbulent days of the land wars to the misty, mysterious regions between history and myth – more than forty stories of old New Zealand by one of our greatest writers and Maori scholars.

THE WONDER BOOK OF MAORI LEGENDS
A. W. Reed
A retelling for children of favourite stories from Maori tradition: the deeds of the demi-god Maui, the heroic adventures of Hatupatu, the romance of Hinemoa and Tutanekai, and many more.

THE CONCISE MAORI DICTIONARY
A. W. Reed, revised by T. S. Karetu
The most up-to-date dictionary with Maori-English and English-Maori sections, containing current words and phrases as well as classical vocabulary and a pronunciation guide.

THE CONCISE MAORI HANDBOOK
A. W. Reed with A. E. Brougham
A compendium volume containing *The Concise Maori Dictionary* and *A Dictionary of Maori Place Names* together with a dictionary of proverbs and an encyclopaedia of traditional life and customs.